Learning Yeoman

Design, implement, and deliver a successful modern web application project using three powerful tools in the Yeoman workflow

Jonathan Spratley

BIRMINGHAM - MUMBAI

Learning Yeoman

First published: August 2014

Production reference: 1120814

Published by Packt Publishing Ltd.
Livery Place
35 Livery Street
Birmingham B3 2PB, UK.

ISBN 978-1-78398-138-0

www.packtpub.com

Cover image by Tony Shi (shihe99@hotmail.com)

Credits

Author
Jonathan Spratley

Reviewers
Lauren Bridge
Dejan Markovic
Matt Momont

Commissioning Editor
Edward Gordon

Acquisition Editors
Sam Birch
Ellen Bishop

Content Development Editor
Rikshith Shetty

Technical Editor
Neha Mankare

Copy Editors
Janbal Dharmaraj
Karuna Narayanan
Alfida Paiva

Project Coordinators
Melita Lobo
Kartik Vedam

Proofreaders
Simran Bhogal
Lauren Harkins
Lawrence Herman
Joanna McMahon

Indexers
Hemangini Bari
Tejal Soni

Graphics
Ronak Dhruv

Production Coordinator
Arvindkumar Gupta

Cover Work
Arvindkumar Gupta

About the Author

Jonathan Spratley, or as his friends call him, Jonnie, is currently working at GE Software and actively uses technologies such as Yo, Bower, Grunt, Node, AngularJS, and Backbone. He leveraged his knowledge of creating Yeoman web applications to write this book. He started developing with HTML, CSS, and JavaScript around 2004 and has spent several years designing and implementing web applications for both mobile and desktop browsers. He is a full-stack developer with experience in both server- and client-side technologies. His passion for tools and technologies that streamline a developer's productivity has driven him to become an autodidact. He has written articles for Safari Books Online Blog, and Flash & Flex Developer's Magazine. This is his first time as an author.

I would like to dedicate this book to all those who believed in me.

About the Reviewers

Lauren Bridge is a software engineer on the Predix platform team at GE Software. She earned her BS in Computer Science from the University of Michigan and is working on her MCS at the University of Illinois at Urbana-Champaign. She mostly develops in JavaScript and Java, and she enjoys learning more frontend web technologies every day.

> I would like to thank Jonnie for teaching me about Yeoman.

Dejan Markovic is an accomplished web developer who enjoys working on both frontend and backend technologies. Since 2003, he has added great value to numerous projects for small- and medium-sized businesses as well as major corporations such as Rogers Media and Softchoice. He is the co-owner of NYTO Group (New York City/Toronto Group), a premium web development company in Toronto, Canada.

NYTO Group's portfolio is available at http://nytogroup.com/portfolio/. NYTO Group is always looking for new projects and partnerships.

Matt Momont is a full-stack developer at GE Software working on the Industrial Internet—the Internet of (really big) Things. He holds a Computer Science degree from the University of Notre Dame and is currently pursuing his Masters in Computer Science at the University of Illinois at Urbana-Champaign. He likes Yeoman because it helps backend developers quickly scaffold out frontend web applications.

www.PacktPub.com

Support files, eBooks, discount offers, and more

You might want to visit www.PacktPub.com for support files and downloads related to your book.

Did you know that Packt offers eBook versions of every book published, with PDF and ePub files available? You can upgrade to the eBook version at www.PacktPub.com and as a print book customer, you are entitled to a discount on the eBook copy. Get in touch with us at service@packtpub.com for more details.

At www.PacktPub.com, you can also read a collection of free technical articles, sign up for a range of free newsletters and receive exclusive discounts and offers on Packt books and eBooks.

http://PacktLib.PacktPub.com

Do you need instant solutions to your IT questions? PacktLib is Packt's online digital book library. Here, you can access, read and search across Packt's entire library of books.

Why subscribe?

- Fully searchable across every book published by Packt
- Copy and paste, print and bookmark content
- On demand and accessible via web browser

Free access for Packt account holders

If you have an account with Packt at www.PacktPub.com, you can use this to access PacktLib today and view nine entirely free books. Simply use your login credentials for immediate access.

Table of Contents

Preface

Now is the time to start using a workflow that can keep up with the fast pace of the development world. Software changes so fast that keeping your project libraries updated and using the latest code has always been a manual, tedious process. Well, not anymore, thanks to modern tooling that has taken my development productivity to greater levels! I have been using Yeoman since the early versions, where Yeoman was the one tool that could do it all.

Since the Yeoman project grew, it has evolved into something I have always wanted in the web development community, such as code generators that can quickly scaffold out working applications that are in alignment with the best practices of that specific framework or language. Now, the time has come and Yeoman is going to take the development world by storm and grow into something that will become a standard in creating modern web applications.

This book is a compilation of using the most popular Yeoman generators on npm. We explore the options that each tool has to offer and use them to create various types of projects, ranging from AngularJS applications to Node.js modules. This book provides examples and information regarding the tools in Yeoman.

What this book covers

Chapter 1, Modern Workflows for Modern Webapps, is an overview of the three core tools used in the Yeoman workflow — Yo, Bower, and Grunt. We cover how to use these tools in development and how to incorporate the workflow into new or existing projects, followed by an example of each of the features in Yeoman.

Chapter 2, Getting Started, begins with installing Yeoman for development and an overview on the AngularJS, Backbone.js, Ember.js, and webapp generators, the options and subgenerators it uses, and examples of using each generator to start the project.

Chapter 3, My Angular Project, starts out with covering the concepts of Angular and the anatomy of an AngularJS application. We will use the generator-angular to scaffold an extendable AngularJS application that uses directives, services, and factories. We will cover setting up a CRUD application with unit tests that use the Karma runner.

Chapter 4, My Backbone Project, covers the anatomy of a Backbone.js project and the concepts behind the library. We create a Backbone application to perform CRUD operations on a data source that is unit tested using Jasmine. The project uses CoffeeScript, Require.js, and AMD to create a well-structured app ready for extending.

Chapter 5, My Ember Project, starts out by creating a new Ember.js project. We then cover how an Ember application is structured and the concepts around the framework, configuring a test environment that is used to run both unit and integration tests.

Chapter 6, Custom Generators, covers the Yeoman generator API and the common methods used when developing generators. We also cover installing and invoking the generator-generator to create a custom Yeoman generator with option prompts that scaffold a custom application based on users' feedback. We cover how to handle testing the generators using nodeunit and then we publish the generator to npm.

Chapter 7, Custom Libraries, covers using Yeoman to create custom libraries that are deployed to either Bower or npm. We learn how to use the Node.js generator and the CommonJS generator to create a Node module, followed by a client-side jQuery plugin that handles sending CRUD operations to a Node REST API server.

Chapter 8, Tasks with Grunt, starts out by covering all the available options when using the Grunt command. We install two Yeoman Grunt generators: the Gruntfile generator that enables adding Grunt to existing projects, and the Grunt plugin generator. We cover creating a custom Grunt task that is then deployed to npm along with unit tests using the nodeunit framework.

Chapter 9, Yeoman Tips and Tricks, aims to cover the holes from the Yeoman generators and specific projects. We cover adding code coverage to a Backbone.js project, as well as setting up Protractor to run end-2-end testing for our Angular project.

What you need for this book

You will need to have the following installed software on your development box in order to properly run the examples and tutorials in the chapters:

- Node 0.10.24
- NPM 1.4.7
- Git 1.8.5.2
- Ruby 1.9.2
- Text editor of some sort
- Google Chrome

Who this book is for

This book is for newbies and intermediate web developers looking to speed up the process when it comes to creating web applications of various frameworks. You should have basic knowledge of HTML, CSS, and JavaScript. The examples in this book will use jQuery style selectors and methods, so some jQuery experience is needed. The tools in this book involve the command line, so having basic knowledge about using the shell to invoke commands on a system is required. As long as you understand basic principles about structuring HTML and OO JavaScript applications, you should have no problem following the step-by-step examples in the chapters.

Conventions

In this book, you will find a number of styles of text that distinguish between different kinds of information. Here are some examples of these styles, and an explanation of their meaning.

Code words in text, database table names, folder names, filenames, file extensions, pathnames, dummy URLs, user input, and Twitter handles are shown as follows: "The `bower.json` file is how Bower manages the project's dependencies."

A block of code is set as follows:

```
<div class="header">
  <ul class="nav nav-pills pull-right">
    <li ng-repeat="item in App.menu"
      ng-class="{'active': App.location.path() === item.href}">
      <a ng-href = "#{{item.href}}"> {{item.title}} </a>
    </li>
  </ul>
  <h3 class="text-muted"> {{ App.sitetitle }} </h3>
</div>
```

When we wish to draw your attention to a particular part of a code block, the relevant lines or items are set in bold:

```
require 'scripts/config'
LearningYeomanCh5 = window.LearningYeomanCh5 =
  Ember.Application.create(
  LOG_VIEW_LOOKUPS: true
  LOG_ACTIVE_GENERATION: true
  LOG_BINDINGS: true
  config: window.Config
)
```

Any command-line input or output is written as follows:

```
$ npm install -g generator-webapp
```

New terms and **important words** are shown in bold. Words that you see on the screen, in menus or dialog boxes for example, appear in the text like this: "See for yourself; open Chrome Developer Tools and click on the **Network** tab."

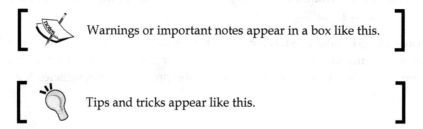

Warnings or important notes appear in a box like this.

Tips and tricks appear like this.

Reader feedback

Feedback from our readers is always welcome. Let us know what you think about this book—what you liked or may have disliked. Reader feedback is important for us to develop titles that you really get the most out of.

To send us general feedback, simply send an e-mail to feedback@packtpub.com, and mention the book title via the subject of your message.

If there is a topic that you have expertise in and you are interested in either writing or contributing to a book, see our author guide on www.packtpub.com/authors.

Customer support

Now that you are the proud owner of a Packt book, we have a number of things to help you to get the most from your purchase.

Downloading the example code

You can download the example code files for all Packt books you have purchased from your account at http://www.packtpub.com. If you purchased this book elsewhere, you can visit http://www.packtpub.com/support and register to have the files e-mailed directly to you.

Errata

Although we have taken every care to ensure the accuracy of our content, mistakes do happen. If you find a mistake in one of our books—maybe a mistake in the text or the code—we would be grateful if you would report this to us. By doing so, you can save other readers from frustration and help us improve subsequent versions of this book. If you find any errata, please report them by visiting http://www.packtpub.com/submit-errata, selecting your book, clicking on the **errata submission form** link, and entering the details of your errata. Once your errata are verified, your submission will be accepted and the errata will be uploaded on our website, or added to any list of existing errata, under the Errata section of that title. Any existing errata can be viewed by selecting your title from http://www.packtpub.com/support.

Piracy

Piracy of copyright material on the Internet is an ongoing problem across all media. At Packt, we take the protection of our copyright and licenses very seriously. If you come across any illegal copies of our works, in any form, on the Internet, please provide us with the location address or website name immediately so that we can pursue a remedy.

Please contact us at copyright@packtpub.com with a link to the suspected pirated material.

We appreciate your help in protecting our authors, and our ability to bring you valuable content.

Questions

You can contact us at questions@packtpub.com if you are having a problem with any aspect of the book, and we will do our best to address it.

1
Modern Workflows for Modern Webapps

This chapter will cover the three core tools that make up the Yeoman workflow, how to use these tools in development, and how to incorporate this workflow into new or existing projects.

In this chapter, you will learn the following topics:

- The Yeoman tools and architecture
- Downloading and installing Yeoman
- Features of Yeoman
- Using the Yeoman tools

An overview of Yeoman

The term **modern webapps** is a relatively new thing, as the Web is still in its infancy stage. As the Web matures, so does the need for developer tools and workflows, thanks to some modern-day Web pioneers over at Google. Paul Irish and Addy Osmani have developed a modern workflow that goes by the name of **Yeoman**.

The Yeoman workflow is a collection of three tools to improve developers' productivity when building web applications: **Yo** is the scaffolding tool, **Grunt** is the build tool, and **Bower** is the package tool.

- Yo is used to scaffold things such as projects and files from templates
- Grunt is used for task management, testing, code linting, and optimization
- Bower is used for package management and to manage client-side dependencies

Yeoman's architecture

The Yeoman toolset runs in the Node.js environment and is invoked from the command line. Each tool is installed using **Node's package manager (npm)** and uses the npm repository to manage all plugins.

Node's package manager

Node.js is a platform that is built on Chrome's JavaScript runtime engine. Node.js uses an event-driven, non-blocking I/O model that makes it lightweight, efficient, and perfect for real-time applications that run across distributed devices.

The official package manager for Node.js is npm. From Node versions 0.6.3 and up, npm is bundled and installed automatically with the environment. The npm package manager runs through the command line and manages the application dependencies that are available on the npm registry.

 The current Node.js version used in this book is v0.10.28.

Features of Yeoman

Before we dig deep into using each tool of the workflow, let's take a look at some of the Yeoman tooling features that will help you in your next project:

- **Quick install**: Easily installs all three tools from the npm repository using one command
- **Scaffolding**: Fast and easy-to-use command-line tool to create new projects or files from templates that individual generators provide
- **Build process**: Tasks for concatenation, minification, optimization, and testing
- **Preview server**: Connect LiveReload server to preview your application in the browser
- **Package management**: Search, install, and manage project dependencies via the command line
- **Code linting**: Scripts are run against JSHint to ensure language best practices
- **Automation**: A simple watch task to compile CoffeeScript, LESS, or SASS, and reload the browser upon changes

- **Testing**: Executes JavaScript code in multiple real browsers with the Karma runner
- **Optimization**: Images are optimized using OptiPNG and JPEGtran, and HTML is optimized using the HTML minifier

The preceding features are dependent on what the individual generators provide via Grunt tasks. By default, the Angular, Backbone, Ember, and other webapp generators provide tasks to perform all the features listed.

 Grunt tasks are individual plugins that perform specific operations on files or folders.

Quick installation

Modern tools usually mean more tools to learn, but learning the tools of the Yeoman workflow is easier than you think. To demonstrate by example, here is how easy it is to get a modern web application up and running, all from the command line.

Installing Yeoman and friends

To install all three tools in the Yeoman workflow, just execute the following command in the terminal:

```
$ npm install -g yo
```

The command will install Yo, Grunt, and Bower into your systems path as follows:

- The -g option flag specifies the installation to be globally available in your path, allowing the yo command to be invoked from anywhere
- If using the latest versions of Node and Git, Yeoman will automatically install Bower and Grunt while installing Yo

 The -g flag installs globally and requires an administrator user.

If you run into any errors during the initial installation process, you can install the envcheck module to ensure that your system is ready for all of Yeoman's features; just execute the following command:

```
$ npm install -g envcheck
```

Installing a generator

To install generators for Yo, use `npm`. Let's install the generic webapp generator; open a terminal and execute the following command:

```
$ npm install -g generator-webapp
```

The preceding command will install the webapp generator globally on your system, easily letting you create new web projects within any directory of your choice.

Scaffolding with Yo

Yeoman includes a powerful command-line utility that can scaffold files based on individual generator templates, allowing you to save time creating files from scratch. There are over 700 community generators on npm.

- To search for generators, add the `generator-` prefix before the name, as follows:

```
$ npm search generator-[name]
```

- To install generators, use `npm install` passing in the name of the package, as follows:

```
$ npm install generator-[name]
```

 The npm attribute is the package manager for Node.js and comes bundled with it.

Creating the project

All Yeoman commands work off the current directory, so create a new folder named `learning-yeoman-ch1`, open the terminal, and `cd` to that location into the newly created directory.

Invoking the generator

Yo, the scaffold tool, will easily create and set up project configuration, files, and folders needed for a modern web application. Execute the following command:

```
$ yo webapp
```

Generators can be invoked with different options; in the preceding command, we use the generators' default options that include Mocha as the test framework and JavaScript as the scripting language. You will get an output similar to the following screenshot:

The preceding command does many things. First off, it's going to ask you a few questions about your new project, such as whether to include Twitter Bootstrap with or without Compass SASS and whether to include Modernizr.

Select the first option (Bootstrap), and press *Enter*; you will see the output to the terminal, and Yeoman is performing all the magic right before your eyes.

Directory structure

Do not be overwhelmed by the number of files generated; take a minute and examine the directory structure that Yeoman produces. You will notice how organized the directory structure is. It looks as follows:

```
├── Gruntfile.js
├── app
│   ├── 404.html
│   ├── bower_components
```

```
|   |      ├── bootstrap
|   |      └── jquery
|   ├── favicon.ico
|   ├── images
|   ├── index.html
|   ├── robots.txt
|   ├── scripts
|   |      └── main.js
|   └── styles
|          └── main.css
├── bower.json
├── node_modules
├── package.json
└── test
       ├── bower.json
       ├── bower_components
       ├── index.html
       └── spec
```

Just think of Yeoman as a helpful robot that does all the hard work for you, creating all the necessary files and folders to get started with development.

The build process

Yeoman includes Grunt, a task-based command-line tool for JavaScript projects. It is used to perform various build tasks on projects and exposes several useful tasks that you will want to use in your workflow. Yeoman automatically creates and configures Gruntfile.js, which specifies the configuration of the tasks and targets.

The following order of commands is used for a seamless development workflow:

```
$ yo webapp                    #scaffold application
$ bower install jquery         #install dependency
$ grunt serve                  #start preview server
$ grunt test                   #run unit tests
$ grunt                        #create optimized build
```

Generally, a modern web developer's workflow consists of the following steps:

1. First, scaffold a new application using yo.
2. Search and install third-party client-side libraries using bower.
3. Start a preview server for development that allows you to write code, save it, and watch the results automatically become refreshed.
4. Then run the test task that executes the tests located in the test directory.
5. Then use the default grunt task to run the tests before creating an optimized build.

To view all the installed grunt tasks associated with the project, you can use the grunt -h command, which will output a list of all tasks and their descriptions.

The Connect LiveReload server

Now that you have all the initial files and folders for the project, you can really start to see the power of Yeoman.

Previewing the server

Connect LiveReload is the module that is a server that will auto reload when files are changed by the watch process.

To preview the application, execute the following command:

```
$ grunt serve
```

The serve task does a few things, which are as follows:

1. First, it removes all the files in the .tmp directory via the clean task.
2. It starts the Connect LiveReload server located at 127.0.0.1:9000, and opens the default web browser via the connect task.
3. Then, finally, it runs the watch task that monitors the project's source (app/*) files, thus executing subtasks on changes.

Your default browser should have opened up, displaying the following page:

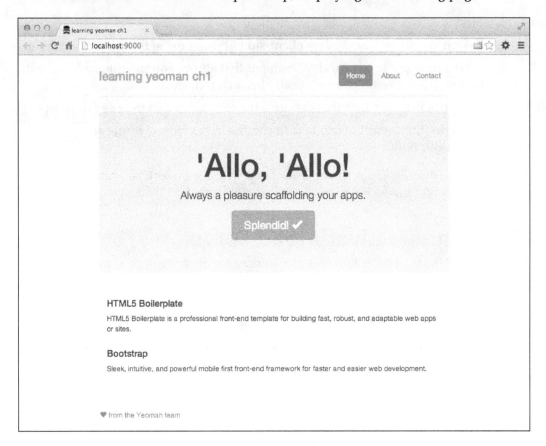

Package management with Bower

Yeoman includes an excellent tool called Bower, which is a package manager for the Web and allows you to easily manage dependencies for your projects. Packages can include any type of assets such as JavaScript, images, and CSS. Twitter and the open source community actively maintain it.

Here are some of the available Bower commands:

- `search`: This command will search for a dependency in the Bower registry
- `install`: This command installs one or more dependencies
- `list`: This command lists all the dependencies installed in the project
- `update`: This command updates a dependency to the latest version

Let's go ahead and add a templating library to our webapp to handle the compilation of model data with HTML for the view. Open the terminal and execute the following command:

```
$ bower install handlebars --save
```

This command will download the Handlebars templating library and place the package in the app/bower_components directory.

To view all client-side dependencies associated with the project, just use the bower list command that will output a tree of all the installed components and their versions, and also inform us if updates are available, as shown in the following screenshot:

```
learning-yeoman-ch1:$ bower list
bower check-new     Checking for new versions of the project dependencies..
learning-yeoman-ch1 /WWW/Learning_Yeoman/learning-yeoman-ch1
├─┬ bootstrap#3.1.1 (latest is 3.2.0)
│ └── jquery#1.11.1 (2.1.1 available)
├── handlebars#1.3.0 (latest is 2.0.0-alpha.4)
└── jquery#1.11.1 (latest is 2.1.1)
learning-yeoman-ch1:$
```

The preceding screenshot is the result of running the bower list command from within the project's root directory or the directory containing the bower.json file, which stores all the installed libraries.

The --save flag tells Bower to write the library name and version to the bower.json file located in the project's root directory. The bower.json file is how Bower manages the project's dependencies.

To wire up the newly downloaded package to the application's index.html page, execute the following grunt task:

```
$ grunt bowerInstall
```

This command will read the contents of the index.html file in the app folder. Then, look for the <!-- bower:js --> block and inject a script tag with the location of the component's main file for each package in the bower_components directory.

Code linting with JSHint

Yeoman includes JSHint, which is a linting tool that helps developers detect errors and potential problems in their JavaScript code; it is a great way to force best practices and improve the code quality. This is very useful when working with a large code base or in a team environment.

The `jshint` task is responsible for linting all code before it gets executed. The following screenshot shows an example of using the `jshint` task. It displays the errors that output when code fails the linking process:

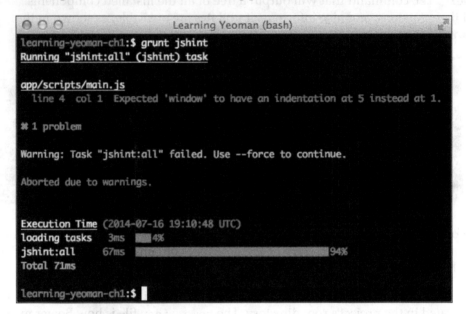

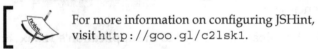 For more information on configuring JSHint, visit http://goo.gl/c21sk1.

Let's begin to add some logic to the applications' main script file that was created during the initial scaffold. Open `app/scripts/main.js` and add the following:

```
/* global Handlebars */
(function () {
  'use strict';
  window.App = {
    init: function (config) {
      console.log( '1 - initialize' );
      this.config = config;
      if (this.config.feature && this.config.feature.endpoint) {
```

```
        this.fetch();
      }
      return this;
    },
    render: function () {
      console.log( '4 - render' );
      var template = Handlebars.compile( $( this.config.el ).find(
        'script[type="text/x-handlebars-template"]' ).html() );
      var html = template( this.config );
      $( this.config.el ).html( html );
      return this;
    },
    onSuccess: function (response) {
      console.log( '3 - onSuccess' );
      this.config.features = response;
      this.render();
    },
    onError: function (error) {
      return this.log( error );
    },
    fetch: function () {
      console.log( '2 - fetch' );
      var self = this;
      $.ajax( {
        url: self.config.feature.endpoint,
        dataType: 'jsonp',
        success: function (results) {
          return self.onSuccess( results );
        },
        error: function (error) {
          return self.onError( error );
        }
      } );
    }
  };
})();

console.log( 'Allo, Allo!' );
```

Here is the breakdown of the preceding code:

1. First, we define Handlebars' global library to let JSHint know what we are doing.

2. Then, we create a new `App` object on the JavaScript global `window` object.

3. The `render` method takes the `config.el` property and renders the compiled template into the element.

4. The `init` function takes a `config` object as the argument and will be set on the class as the `config` property.

5. If the passed object has a `feature.endpoint` property, then the app will fetch `features` from that endpoint.

6. The `render` method will compile the Handlebars template with the `config` object to create the HTML output, which is injected into `config.el`.

7. The `onSuccess` method will set the `model.features` property to the `results` of the request and invoke the `render` method to display the contents.

8. The `onError` method will log the error to the console.

9. The `fetch` method will invoke a JSONP request to `config.feature.endpoint`.

Save the file, and the lint task will then compile into JavaScript and reload the browser; nothing will look different because we haven't added the application's template.

Automation

Yeoman comes with a `watch` task that is responsible for the automation of different tasks when developing web applications, such as compiling CoffeeScript to JavaScript when source files change or concatenating and parsing SASS files and then reloading the web browser to see changes.

The automation tasks are limited to the Grunt tasks that are defined by the generator; any changes to the `.js` or `.html` file in the `app` directory will automatically get parsed, and the browser will get refreshed. If the `watch` task detects changes to files in the `test` directory, then the unit tests are run via the `test` task.

Let's create the application's template; we will use the {{ }} double mustache syntax to render the dynamic content. Open the `app/index.html` file, and add the following contents inside the `body` element right below the `browsehappy` code line:

```
...
<![endif]-->
  <div class="container">
```

```
<script type="text/x-handlebars-template">
  <div class="header">
    <ul class="nav nav-pills pull-right">
      <li class="active">
        <a href="/">Home</a>
      </li>
      {{#each menu}}
      <li>
        <a href="#{{route}}">{{name}}</a>
      </li>
      {{/each}}
    </ul>
    <h3 class="text-muted">{{sitetitle}}</h3>
  </div>
  <div class="jumbotron">
    <h1>{{feature.title}}</h1>
    <img src="{{feature.image}}"/>
    <p class="lead">{{feature.body}}</p>
  </div>
  <div class="marketing">
    {{#each features}}
    <div class="media">
      <a class="pull-left">
        <img src="{{ image }}" class="img-thumbnail"/>
      </a>
      <div class="media-body">
        <h4 class="media-heading">{{ title }}</h4>
        <p>{{ body }}</p>
      </div>
    </div>
    {{/ each }}
  </div>
  <div class="footer">
    <p>{{sitecopy}}</p>
  </div>
</script>
</div>
<!-- build:js scripts/vendor.js -->
```

The preceding code is very similar to the HTML that was created by Yeoman, except we are replacing the static content with data for Handlebars to compile the template with dynamic configuration data. Now, let's initialize the application by adding the following script block at the bottom of the `app/index.html` file in the `app` folder that was created during the initial scaffold:

```html
<!-- build:js({app,.tmp}) scripts/main.js -->
<script src="scripts/main.js"></script>
<!-- endbuild -->
<script>
  $(document).ready(function() {
    App.init({
      el: '.container',
      sitetitle : 'Learning Yeoman',
      sitecopy : '2014 Copyright',
      version: '0.0.1',
      feature : {
        title : 'Chapter 1',
        body : 'a starting point for a modern web app.',
        image : 'http://goo.gl/kZZ6dX',
        endpoint :
          'http://jonniespratley.me:8181/api/v2/learning-yeoman-
          ch1/posts'
      },
      features : null,
      menu: [
        {name: 'About', route: '/about'},
        {name: 'Contact', route: '/contact'}
      ]
    });
  });
</script>
```

In the preceding code, we perform the following steps:

1. First, we use jQuery's `ready` method to wait for the document to finish loading before executing the contents.

2. Then, a new instance of the `App` class is created, passing in the site configuration options.

3. The `endpoint` property is set to a simple API endpoint used to access the `features` data.

4. The `el` property is set to the `div.container` element in the `index.html` page.

5. Then, general site information such as the title, version, and copyright is declared.

6. The site feature information is populated with default content, and the site navigation menu array is defined with two items that represent pages.

7. Save the file, and you will see your browser automatically reloading with something similar to the following screenshot:

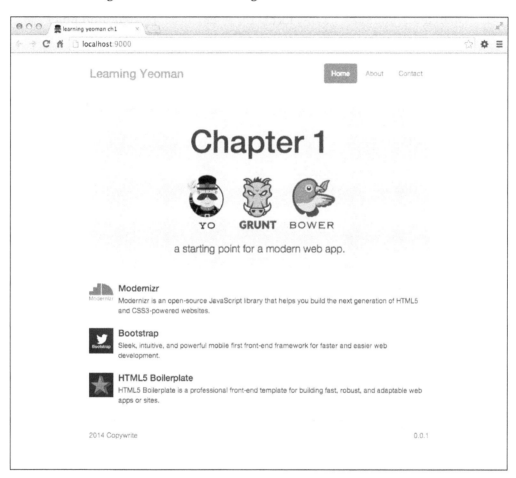

Testing with PhantomJS

If testing is not a part of your workflow, it should be! Yeoman makes it incredibly easy to test your application by setting up a testing environment with the Mocha framework. Other options include Jasmine, QUnit, and just about any other framework. That helpful robot (Yeoman) just saved hours of development time by creating all the necessary configuration files during the initial project scaffold.

Several testing tasks can be customized to do many useful things like showing test results in JUnit for use in many continuous integration systems such as Jenkins and Bamboo. Perform the following steps:

1. Open the `Gruntfile.js` file, locate the `mocha` task object around line #138, and configure the specific options for this target, as follows:

```
...
//#138 - Mocha testing framework configuration options
mocha: {
  all: {
    options: {
      run: true,
      log: true,
      reporter: 'Spec',
      files: ['<%= config.app %>/scripts/{,*/}*.js']
    }
  }
},
...
```

In the preceding code:

  ◦ We specify where the source of the scripts are by the `files` property

  ◦ The `run` and `log` properties, as you may have guessed, log the output and run the tests

  ◦ The `reporter` property is `Spec`, so it will display the message in the console

2. Then, the `files` property sets the location of the test specs. Open the default test the generator created, `test/spec/test.js`, and add the following:

```
/*global App, expect, it, describe */
'use strict';
var testApp = null;
var config = {
  el: '.container',
  sitetitle: 'Learning Yeoman',
```

```
    sitecopy: '2014 Copyright',
    version: '0.0.1',
    feature: {
      title: 'Chapter 1',
      body: 'a starting point for a modern web application.',
      image: 'http://goo.gl/kZZ6dX',
      endpoint: '/posts'
    },
    features: null
  };
  testApp = App.init( config );
  describe( 'Learning Yeoman Chapter 1 Test', function () {
    describe( 'App.init', function () {
      it( 'should store config on instance',
        function (done) {
          expect( testApp.config.version, 'App.config'
            ).to.equal( config.version );
          done();
      } );
    } );
  } );
```

In the preceding code:

   ° First, the JShint configuration at the top defines global variables used in the spec

   ° The `describe` block contains some local variables that define the application's configuration

   ° The `it` block is testing if the configuration options passed to the `App.init` method are correctly set on the `config` property of the `testApp` instance

Running tests

To run the tests, use the following command:

```
$ grunt test
```

The output in the console should look similar to the following screenshot:

```
⊖ ○ ○                    Learning Yeoman (bash)
  Learning Yeoman Chapter 1 Test
    App.init
      ✓ should store config on instance


  1 passing (203ms)

>> 1 passed! (0.20s)

Done, without errors.


Execution Time (2014-06-30 16:38:43 UTC)
concurrent:test    1.4s  ████████████████████39%
autoprefixer:dist  77ms  █2%
mocha:all          2s    ███████████████████████████58%
Total 3.5s

learning-yeoman-ch1:$ grunt test
```

As we can see from the output, the configuration of PhantomJS is already taken care of. It nicely starts the PhantomJS browser; after connecting to the browser, it logs the output to the console as the tests run.

Optimizing for production

The default Grunt task (`$ grunt`) takes care of optimizing your entire project by doing the following:

- Compiles and concatenates all style sheets together
- Minifies all referenced third-party libraries into a separate file
- Groups Angular modules into a separate minimized file
- Then, it combines all application scripts into one separate file
- All HTML files and images are processed through their corresponding optimizer
- All processed files have a revision number appended to the filename
- All built files are located in the `dist` directory, making your application ready for deployment

- To preview what your application runs like once optimized, execute the following command:

```
$ grunt serve:dist
```

- Your webapp is fully optimized with fewer requests; now, it loads much faster in the browser, as shown in the following screenshot:

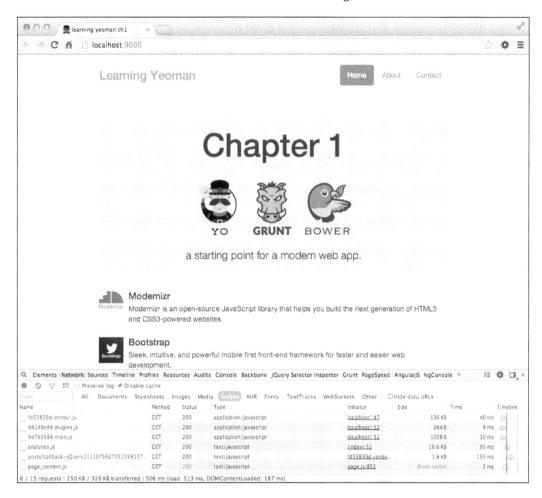

See for yourself; open Chrome Developer Tools and click on the **Network** tab.

Self-test questions

The following are some questions that you should be able to answer after reading this chapter. If you get stuck on a question, the answers are located in the Appendix.

1. Which four Yeoman generators are the most popular among the community?
2. What are the three core tools used in Yeoman?
3. What is the general developer tool workflow when using Yeoman?
4. Which platform and environment does Yeoman run in?
5. Who created Yeoman?

Summary

That was a lot to take in for the first chapter, but we have much more to cover. In this chapter, we learned how to install all the tools in the Yeoman workflow with one easy command: `npm install yo -g`. We learned about the commands that the Bower, Grunt, and Yo webapp generators have to offer. We also got to see the LiveReload server in action while making changes to the generated files.

We were able to make sure our coding syntax was error-free via JSHint. We also got our hands dirty configuring the `mocha` task and a unit test to make sure the app is functioning properly; we wrapped it up by taking a look at the optimization that takes place when your project is ready to ship.

Next, we are going to turn it up a notch by introducing the most popular Yeoman generators in the community: the Angular, Backbone, and Ember generators.

2
Getting Started

This chapter is going to cover getting started with Yeoman generators. We will explore the four most popular official generators, their options and the subgenerators they expose, and the purpose of using them. This chapter is going to cover the following topics:

- The basics of the Yeoman workflow
- Installing the following commonly-used official generators:
  - The **generator-webapp**: This is used to create a generic web application
  - The **generator-angular**: This is used to create an AngularJS web application
  - The **generator-backbone**: This is used to create a Backbone.js web application
  - The **generator-ember**: This is used to create an Ember.js web application
- The subgenerators that these modules expose
- We do not cover any of the grunt tasks that are configured with the projects after they are scaffolded
- The life cycle of creation to deployment using these generators

Yo – generators

What makes Yeoman amazing are the **generators**. There is a robust set of templates (commonly referred to as generators) for any type of project. Finding a generator to install and use is quite simple as well; just use the `npm search generator-[name]` command to search for a generator where the name matches.

The Yeoman workflow

The general workflow to follow when using Yo, Bower, and Grunt is as follows:

1. Install a generator as follows:

    ```
    $ npm install generator-[name]
    ```

2. Scaffold a project:

    ```
    $ yo [generator] [args] [options]
    ```

3. Install a dependency:

    ```
    $ bower install [dependency#version] [options]
    ```

4. Test the project:

    ```
    $ grunt test
    ```

5. Preview the project:

    ```
    $ grunt serve
    ```

6. Build the project for deployment:

    ```
    $ grunt
    ```

Official generators

Here is a list of the official generators maintained by the Yeoman team. Use these as a base to create a custom generator or to create a project:

*   **polymer**: This is a generator used to create Polymer webapps and components
*   **chromeapp**: This is a generator used to create a Google Chrome application
*   **jquery**: This is a generator used to create a custom jQuery library
*   **gruntfile**: This is a generator used to create a basic Gruntfile
*   **commonjs**: This is a generator used to create a CommonJS module, including nodeunit unit tests
*   **nodejs**: This is a generator used to create a Node.js module, including nodeunit unit tests

Other generators include webapp, angular, backbone, ember, jasmine, karma, mocha, bootstrap, mobile, gruntplugin, and chrome-extension.

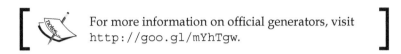 For more information on official generators, visit `http://goo.gl/mYhTgw`.

The generator-webapp

The generator-webapp is the webapp generator for Yeoman that scaffolds a generic web application, including unit testing.

Features

The generator-webapp has some great features worth noting, which include the following:

- It automatically wires up Bower components with the `bower-install` task
- It provides Mocha or Jasmine unit testing with PhantomJS
- It contains Twitter Bootstrap for **Syntactically Awesome Stylesheets** (**SASS**)
- It provides an optimized Modernizr build

Installing the generator-webapp

To use this generator, all that is required is the module installation. This is easily done with the **Node package manager** (**npm**). To install it, use the following command:

```
$ npm install -g generator-webapp
```

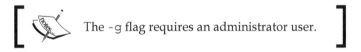 The `-g` flag requires an administrator user.

Using the generator-webapp

The following is how the generator-webapp is invoked from the command line:

```
$ yo webapp [name] [options]
```

Options

The webapp generator has the following options available:

Option	Description	Defaults
--skip-install	Skips automatic execution of Bower and npm	False
--test-framework	Sets the testing framework	Mocha
--coffee	Enables support for CoffeeScript	False

[These options are applied during the initial project's scaffold.]

Example usage

To use the generator, simply open a terminal and execute the following:

```
$ yo webapp hello-webapp
```

The preceding command will scaffold a new webapp project with the name hello-webapp.

You will be prompted to answer some questions that the generator asks, such as whether to:

- Use SASS with Compass
- Include Twitter Bootstrap
- Include Modernizer

After answering these questions, the project files are created, the dependencies are downloaded and installed into the bower_components directory, and the application is ready to preview.

Previewing

To run the application, you can use the following command to start the server and open a default web browser that displays the application:

```
$ grunt serve
```

On opening, your default web browser should display a page similar to the following screenshot:

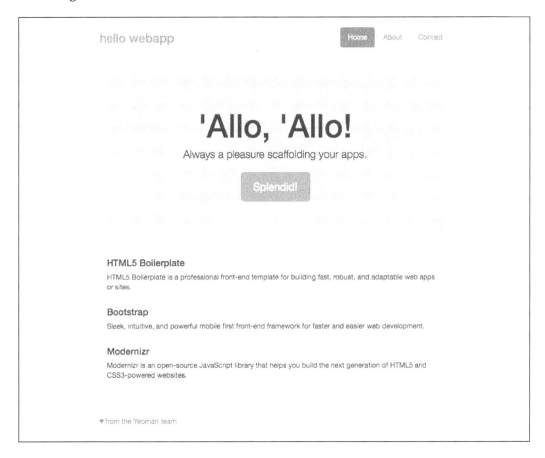

Conclusion

Typically, one will want to consider using the webapp generator when looking to create a scaffold out of a simple website that can be easily deployed to Heroku or another cloud application server for hosting.

The generator-angular

This is the AngularJS generator for Yeoman, which quickly scaffolds a new project with sensible defaults and community best practices. This is one of the most popular generators in the community, with more forks and stars on Github than any other.

Features

Some notable features that the generator-angular includes are as follows:

- It is based on the angular-seed project
- It includes ngCookies, ngSanitize, ngResource, and ngRoute modules
- It includes Twitter Bootstrap with or without SASS
- It provides full CoffeeScript support

Installing the generator-angular

The following command is used to install the AngularJS generator:

```
$ npm install -g generator-angular
```

 The -g flag requires an administrator user.

Using the generator-angular

This is how to use this new generator:

```
$ yo angular[:subgenerator] [args] [options]
```

Options

The following options are available when invoking the generator-angular:

Option	Description	Defaults
--help	Prints the generator's options and usage	False
--app-suffix	Allows a custom suffix to be added to the module name	False
--coffee	Generates CoffeeScript instead of JavaScript	False
--minsafe	Generates AngularJS minification safe code	False

Example usage

The following is an example of using the generator to create a new AngularJS application:

```
$ yo angular hello-angular
```

The preceding command will invoke the generator with the application name set to `hello-angular`.

Angular subgenerators

The following subgenerators are provided with the generator-angular; all of the subgenerators listed as follows can run independently:

- `angular:app`: The `angular` or `angular:app` command is used to create the initial AngularJS application. This is shown in the following code:

  ```
  $ yo angular:app [name]
  ```

- `angular:common`: The `angular:common` subgenerator is used to create the general default files used for an AngularJS application. This is shown in the following code:

  ```
  $ yo angular:common [name]
     create app/scripts/services/[name].js
  ```

- `angular:constant`: The `angular:constant` subgenerator is used to create a module that is available during the configuration and run phases of the application's life cycle, which Angular cannot override. This is shown in the following code:

  ```
  $ yo angular:constant [name]
     create app/scripts/services/[name].js
     create test/spec/services/[name].js
  ```

- `angular:decorator`: The `angular:decorator` subgenerator is used to create a decorator module that can be used to intercept the creation of a service, allowing methods to be overridden or modified during the configuration phase of the services' life cycle. This is shown in the following code:

  ```
  $ yo angular:decorator [name]
  ```

- `angular:directive`: The `angular:directive` subgenerator is used to create an Angular directive. This module allows you to create reusable view components for the application. This is shown in the following code:

  ```
  $ yo angular:directive [name]
     create app/scripts/directives/[name].js
     create test/spec/directives/[name].js
  ```

- `angular:factory`: The `angular:factory` subgenerator is used to create an Angular factory. This module can be used to create reusable pieces of the application logic. This is shown in the following code:

```
$ yo angular:factory [name]
    create app/scripts/services/[name].js
    create test/spec/services/[name].js
```

- `angular:main`: The `angular:main` subgenerator is used to create the main Angular module used to Bootstrap an Angular application and configure the router. This is shown in the following code:

```
$ yo angular:main [name]
```

- `angular:provider`: The `angular:provider` subgenerator is used to create an Angular provider module used to expose an API for application-wide configuration that must be made before the application starts. This is shown in the following code:

```
$ yo angular:provider [name]
```

- `angular:route`: The `angular:route` subgenerator is used to create an Angular view template and controller, and add a route to the application's router. This module allows you to handle the routes for the application. This is shown in the following code:

```
$ yo angular:route [name]
    create app/scripts/controllers/[name].js
    create test/spec/controllers/[name].js
    create app/views/[name].html
```

- `angular:service`: The `angular:service` subgenerator is used to create an Angular service module. This module allows you to create reusable business logic for the application. This is shown in the following code:

```
$ yo angular:service [name]
    create app/scripts/services/[name].js
    create test/spec/services/[name].js
```

- `angular:value`: The `angular:value` subgenerator is used to create an Angular value module. This module allows you to define simple objects or strings for the application. This is shown in the following code:

```
$ yo angular:value [name]
```

- angular:view: The angular:view subgenerator is used to create an Angular view template. This template allows you to use AngularJS directives and data-binding syntax to display data from the controllers' scope.

```
$ yo angular:view [name]
    create app/views/[name].html
```

Previewing

To run the application, you use the serve task to start the preview server, which opens a default web browser that displays the application; append :dist to start the server in the distribution mode. For example, to run the application execute the following command:

```
$ grunt serve
```

After running the command, your default web browser should display a page similar to the following screenshot:

This is the example running in serve mode; the `watch` task is running in the background, enabling changes to LiveReload upon save; give it a try and modify the source file.

Conclusion

The generator-angular is a great generator used to create new AngularJS projects that are already preconfigured to build, test, and run with minimal effort for the developer.

The generator-backbone

The Backbone.js generator for Yeoman provides a functional boilerplate application out of the box. It includes access to a number of subgenerators that can be easily used to create individual models, views, collections, and routers.

Features

Some notable features that the generator-backbone includes are as follows:

- Require.js (AMD) support
- Full CoffeeScript support
- R.js build optimization of all AMD modules (the Require.js option)
- Unit testing with PhantomJS

Installing the generator-backbone

The following is the command used to install the Backbone.js generator for Yeoman:

```
$ npm install -g generator-backbone
```

 The -g flag requires an administrator user.

Using the generator-backbone

The following shows how to use this new generator:

```
$ yo backbone[:subgenerator] [args] [options]
```

Options

Here are the options available when invoking the Backbone generator:

Option	Description	Defaults
--appPath	Scaffolds into a custom directory	Null
--coffee	Enables scaffolds in CoffeeScript	Null
--requirejs	Scaffolds using Require.js (AMD) loader	Check for Require.js
--skip-install	Skips the automatic execution of Bower and npm	False
--test-framework	Sets the default testing framework	Mocha
--template-framework	Sets the default template framework	Lodash

Example usage

Here, you can see an example of using the Backbone.js generator to create a new project:

```
$ yo backbone hello-backbone
```

In this command, the `backbone` generator is invoked with `hello-backbone` as the application name.

Backbone subgenerators

The following subgenerators are provided with the generator-backbone module:

- The `backbone:app` subgenerator is used to create new Backbone applications. This is shown in the following code:

  ```
  $ yo backbone:app myApp
  ```

- The `backbone:all` subgenerator is used to create a Backbone model, collection, view, route, and template for the passed parameter. This is shown in the following code:

  ```
  $ yo backbone:all tags
    create app/scripts/models
    create app/scripts/collections
    create app/scripts/views
    create app/scripts/routes
    create app/scripts/helpers
    create app/scripts/templates
  ```

- The `backbone:model` subgenerator is used to create new Backbone models for the application. The `Backbone.Model` class provides a set of basic methods and events such as `change`, `invalid`, `destroy`, and `add` to manage changes to data. This is shown in the following code:

```
$ yo backbone:model post

  create app/scripts/models/post.coffee
```

- The `backbone:collection` subgenerator is used to create new Backbone collections for the application. The `Backbone.Collection` class is an ordered set of models and has methods to manage collections of model data. This is shown in the following code:

```
$ yo backbone:collection posts

  create app/scripts/collections/posts.coffee
```

- The `backbone:view` subgenerator is used to create new Backbone views for the application. The `Backbone.View` class provides an organized structure to add custom event handlers that model data and the logic in the view. They render to display the model or collect data. This is shown in the following code:

```
$ yo backbone:view posts

  create app/scripts/templates/posts.ejs

  create app/scripts/views/posts.coffee
```

- The `backbone:router` subgenerator is used to create new Backbone routers for the application. The `Backbone.Router` class provides a set of methods for handling the routing in a client-side web application by connecting (#/route) routes to actions and methods.

```
$ yo backbone:router posts

  create app/scripts/routes/posts.coffee
```

Previewing

To run the application, you can use the `grunt serve` task command to start the preview server and open a default web browser that displays the application; append `:dist` to the view in the production mode. This is shown in the following code:

```
$ grunt serve
```

The following screenshot is the `hello-backbone` example that runs in the serve mode. This is the default layout that is created during the initial scaffold:

Conclusion

The best way to get started with Backbone applications is definitely to use the generator-backbone Yeoman generator. It takes all the pain out of creating a new Require.js Backbone application, with unit testing and R.js optimized build configuration already set up.

The generator-ember

The generator-ember generator handles creating Ember applications; it is based on the Ember.js starter app as the base application.

Features

Some notable features that the generator-ember includes are as follows:

- Optional CoffeeScript support
- Unit testing with Karma and PhantomJS
- Jasmine or Mocha test framework

Installing the generator-ember

This is how to install the Ember.js generator for Yeoman:

```
$ npm install -g generator-ember
```

Using the generator-ember

To use the generator, simply open a console and execute the following:

```
$ yo ember [name] [options]
```

Options

These are the options available when invoking the Ember generator:

Option	Description	Defaults
--coffee	Generates scaffolds in CoffeeScript	False
--skip-install	Skips the automatic execution of Bower and npm	False
--test-framework	Enables different testing frameworks like Jasmine	Mocha
--karma	Enables support for the Karma test runner	Null

Example usage

Here, you can see an example that uses the Ember.js generator to create a new application:

```
$ yo ember hello-ember
```

In this command, the `ember` generator is invoked with `hello-ember` as the app name.

You will be prompted with some questions that the generator asks. After you have answered the questions, and the installation of the project dependencies is complete, you can then preview your new application by running it.

Ember subgenerators

The subgenerators that the Ember generator includes are as follows:

- The `ember:app` subgenerator is used to create the initial Ember application. The `Ember.Application` class helps to instantiate, initialize, and coordinate the objects in the app. This is shown as follows:

  ```
  $ yo ember:app myApp
  ```

  Each Ember project has one and only one `Ember.Application`. This object is created during the initial scaffold of the generator and is the name of the project's folder.

- The `ember:model` subgenerator is used to create a new Ember model. The `DS.Model` class is an object that stores a persisted state; templates use models to display data to the user. This is shown as follows:

  ```
  $ yo ember:model book
      create app/scripts/models/book_model.js
      create      app/scripts/controllers/books_controller.js
      create      app/scripts/controllers/book_edit_controller.js
      create      app/scripts/routes/books_route.js
      create      app/scripts/routes/book_route.js
      create      app/scripts/routes/book_edit_route.js
      create          app/scripts/views/book_view.js
      create          app/scripts/views/book_edit_view.js
      create          app/scripts/views/books_view.js
      create          app/templates/book.hbs
      create          app/templates/book/edit.hbs
      create          app/templates/books.hbs
      create          app/scripts/router.js
  ```

- The `ember:router` subgenerator is used to create a new Ember router. The `Ember.Router` class manages the application state and URLs. This is shown as follows:

  ```
  $ yo ember:router books
      create app/scripts/router.js
  ```

- The `ember:view` subgenerator is used to create a new Ember view. The `Ember.View` class manages the combining of model data with templates and responds to user events. This is shown as follows:

```
$ yo ember:view library
    create app/scripts/views/library_view.js
    create app/scripts/views/library_edit_view.js
    create app/scripts/views/libraries_view.js
    create app/templates/library.hbs
    create app/templates/library/edit.hbs
    create app/templates/libraries.hbs
```

Previewing

To run the application, you can use the following command to start the server and open a default web browser that displays the application; you can use the `serve:dist` task to the view in the production mode:

```
$ grunt serve
```

On opening, your default web browser should display a page that looks similar to the following screenshot:

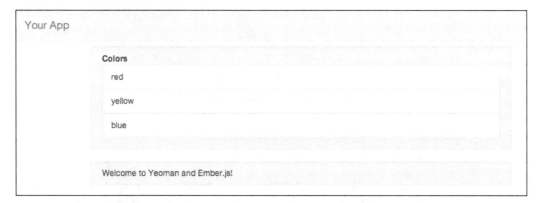

Conclusion

The Ember.js generator is built off the `ember-app` boilerplate and is a great start for development. Something worth noting is that the subgenerators always generate CRUD-type application files and do not allow much customization. Further features are on the road map, which will hopefully solve some of these issues.

Self-test questions

The following are questions you should be able to answer at the end of this chapter:

1. What are the names of at least three official Yeoman generators?
2. Which Angular subgenerator creates a view and a controller, and wires the application's router?
3. Which is the default test framework for the Backbone generator?
4. Which option is common among the four most popular Yeoman generators?
5. Which command is used to search for only Yeoman generators?
6. Which Ember subgenerator will create a model, controller, route, view, and template?
7. Which is the default test framework for the Ember generator?

Summary

In this chapter, we covered the installation and usage of the four most popular official Yeoman generators:

*   The generator-webapp
*   The generator-angular
*   The generator-backbone
*   The generator-ember

We also covered using the subgenerators of each generator to assist in creating various parts of an application in the desired framework.

In the next chapter, we are going to use the AngularJS generator in detail. We will explore each subgenerator, and create the individual pieces of a single page CRUD application. We'll also explore writing unit tests for each of the AngularJS modules as well as setting up an end-to-end test environment to automate the functionality of the application.

3
My Angular Project

AngularJS is a client-side MV* JavaScript framework with tons of features that give web applications structure with two-way data binding and declarative markup, allowing an ease in development of any type of application.

This chapter is going to cover how to use the Angular Yeoman generator to create a single page application that can be easily extended into something more. We will use the angular subgenerators to create the pieces of the application, giving you insight into using the angular generator in a real world project today.

By the end of this chapter, you should have a firm understanding of AngularJS's core concepts and how it fits into a modern web application.

In this chapter, we are going to cover the following:

- Concepts of AngularJS and how to leverage the framework in a new or existing project

- Using the different angular subgenerators to create a CRUD application that uses custom filters, directives, and services

- Getting acquainted with how an AngularJS application is structured using the Yeoman Angular generator

Anatomy of an Angular project

Generally in a **single page application** (**SPA**), you create modules that contain a set of functionality, such as a view to display data, a model to store data, and a controller to manage the relationship between the two. Angular incorporates the basic principles of the MVC pattern into how it builds client-side web applications.

The major Angular concepts are as follows:

- **Templates**: A template is used to write plain HTML with the use of directives and JavaScript expressions

- **Directives**: A directive is a reusable component that extends HTML with the custom attributes and elements

- **Models**: A model is the data that is displayed to the user and manipulated by the user

- **Scopes**: A scope is the context in which the model is stored and made available to controllers, directives, and expressions

- **Expressions**: An expression allows access to variables and functions defined on the scope

- **Filters**: A filter formats data from an expression for visual display to the user

- **Views**: A view is the visual representation of a model displayed to the user, also known as the **Document Object Model (DOM)**

- **Controllers**: A controller is the business logic that manages the view

- **Injector**: The injector is the dependency injection container that handles all dependencies

- **Modules**: A module is what configures the injector by specifying what dependencies the module needs

- **Services**: A service is a piece of reusable business logic that is independent of views

- **Compiler**: The compiler handles parsing templates and instantiating directives and expressions

- **Data binding**: Data binding handles keeping model data in sync with the view

Why Angular?

AngularJS is an open source JavaScript framework known as the **Superheroic JavaScript MVC Framework**, which is actively maintained by the folks over at Google. Angular attempts to minimize the effort in creating web applications by teaching the browser's new tricks. This enables the developers to use declarative markup (known as directives or expressions) to handle attaching the custom logic behind DOM elements.

Angular includes many built-in features that allow easy implementation of the following:

- Two-way data binding in views using double mustaches {{ }}
- DOM control for repeating, showing, or hiding DOM fragments
- Form submission and validation handling
- Reusable HTML components with self-contained logic
- Access to RESTful and JSONP API services

The major benefit of Angular is the ability to create individual modules that handle specific responsibilities, which come in the form of directives, filters, or services. This enables developers to leverage the functionality of the custom modules by passing in the name of the module in the dependencies.

Creating a new Angular project

Now it is time to build a web application that uses some of Angular's features. The application that we will be creating will be based on the scaffold files created by the Angular generator; we will add functionality that enables CRUD operations on a database.

Installing the generator-angular

To install the Yeoman Angular generator, execute the following command:

```
$ npm install -g generator-angular
```

 For Karma testing, the generator-karma needs to be installed.

Scaffolding the application

To scaffold a new AngularJS application, create a new folder named `learning-yeoman-ch3` and then open a terminal in that location. Then, execute the following command:

```
$ yo angular --coffee
```

This command will invoke the AngularJS generator to scaffold an AngularJS application, and the output should look similar to the following screenshot:

```
 ● ○ ○                    Learning Yeoman (node)                    ⬈
learning-yeoman-ch3:$ yo angular --coffee

     .------.
    |      |
    |--(o)--|      .---------------------------.
    `---------´    |    Welcome to Yeoman,      |
   ( _´U`_ )       |    ladies and gentlemen!   |
   /___A___\       '---------------------------'
    |  ~  |
  __'.___.'__
 ´   `  |° ´ Y `

Out of the box I include Bootstrap and some AngularJS recommended modules.

[?] Would you like to use Sass (with Compass)? No
[?] Would you like to include Bootstrap? Yes
[?] Which modules would you like to include? (Press <space> to select)
>● angular-animate.js
 ● angular-cookies.js
 ● angular-resource.js
 ● angular-route.js
 ● angular-sanitize.js
 ● angular-touch.js
```

Understanding the directory structure

Take a minute to become familiar with the directory structure of an Angular application created by the Yeoman generator:

- app: This folder contains all of the front-end code, HTML, JS, CSS, images, and dependencies:

    ○ images: This folder contains images for the application

    ○ scripts: This folder contains AngularJS codebase and business logic:

        ○ app.coffee: This contains the application module definition and routing

        ○ controllers: Custom controllers go here:

            ○ main.coffee: This is the main controller created by default

        ○ directives: Custom directives go here

        ○ filters: Custom filters go here

- ○ `services`: Reusable application services go here
- ○ `styles`: This contains all CSS/LESS/SASS files:
  - ○ `main.css`: This is the main style sheet created by default
- ○ `views`: This contains the HTML templates used in the application
  - ○ `main.html`: This is the main view created by default
- ○ `index.html`: This is the applications' entry point

- `bower_components`: This folder contains client-side dependencies
- `node_modules`: This contains all project dependencies as node modules
- `test`: This contains all the tests for the application:
  - ○ `spec`: This contains unit tests mirroring structure of the `app/scripts` folder
  - ○ `karma.conf.coffee`: This file contains the Karma runner configuration

- `Gruntfile.js`: This file contains all project tasks
- `package.json`: This file contains project information and dependencies
- `bower.json`: This file contains frontend dependency settings

 The directories (`directives`, `filters`, and `services`) get created when the subgenerator is invoked.

Configuring the application

Let's go ahead and create a configuration file that will allow us to store the application wide properties; we will use the Angular value services to reference the configuration object.

Open up a terminal and execute the following command:

```
$ yo angular:value Config
```

This command will create a configuration service located in the `app/scripts/services` directory. This service will store global properties for the application.

 For more information on Angular services, visit `http://goo.gl/Q3f6AZ`.

Now, let's add some settings to the file that we will use throughout the application. Open the `app/scripts/services/config.coffee` file and replace with the following code:

```coffee
'use strict'
angular.module('learningYeomanCh3App').value('Config', Config =
  baseurl: document.location.origin
  sitetitle: 'learning yeoman'
  sitedesc: 'The tutorial for Chapter 3'
  sitecopy: '2014 Copyright'
  version: '1.0.0'
  email: 'jonniespratley@gmail.com'
  debug: true
  feature:
    title: 'Chapter 3'
    body: 'A starting point for a modern angular.js application.'
    image: 'http://goo.gl/YHBZjc'
  features: [
    title: 'yo'
    body: 'yo scaffolds out a new application.'
    image: 'http://goo.gl/g6LO99'
  ,
    title: 'Bower'
    body: 'Bower is used for dependency management.'
    image: 'http://goo.gl/GpxBAx'
  ,
    title: 'Grunt'
    body: 'Grunt is used to build, preview and test your project.'
    image: 'http://goo.gl/9M00hx'
  ]
  session:
    authorized: false
    user: null
  layout:
    header: 'views/_header.html'
    content: 'views/_content.html'
    footer: 'views/_footer.html'
  menu: [
    title: 'Home', href: '/'
  ,
    title: 'About', href: '/about'
  ,
    title: 'Posts', href: '/posts'
  ]
)
```

The preceding code does the following:

- It creates a new `Config` value service on the `learningYeomanCh3App` module
- The `baseURL` property is set to the location where the document originated from
- The `sitetitle`, `sitedesc`, `sitecopy`, and `version` attributes are set to default values that will be displayed throughout the application
- The `feature` property is an object that contains some defaults for displaying a feature on the main page
- The `features` property is an array of feature objects that will display on the main page as well
- The `session` property is defined with `authorized` set to `false` and `user` set to `null`; this value gets set to the current authenticated user
- The `layout` property is an object that defines the paths of view templates, which will be used for the corresponding keys
- The `menu` property is an array that contains the different pages of the application

 Usually, a generic configuration file is created at the top level of the `scripts` folder for easier access.

Creating the application definition

During the initial scaffold of the application, an `app.coffee` file is created by Yeoman located in the `app/scripts` directory. The `scripts/app.coffee` file is the definition of the application, the first argument is the name of the module, and the second argument is an array of dependencies, which come in the form of angular modules and will be injected into the application upon page load.

The `app.coffee` file is the main entry point of the application and does the following:

- Initializes the application module with dependencies
- Configures the applications router

Any module dependencies that are declared inside the dependencies array are the Angular modules that were selected during the initial scaffold. Consider the following code:

```
'use strict'
angular.module('learningYeomanCh3App', [
  'ngCookies',
```

```
    'ngResource',
    'ngSanitize',
    'ngRoute'
  ])
    .config ($routeProvider) ->
      $routeProvider
        .when '/',
          templateUrl: 'views/main.html'
          controller: 'MainCtrl'
        .otherwise
          redirectTo: '/'
```

The preceding code does the following:

- It defines an angular module named learningYeomanCh3App with dependencies on the ngCookies, ngSanitize, ngResource, and ngRoute modules

- The .config function on the module configures the applications' routes by passing route options to the $routeProvider service

 Bower downloaded and installed these modules during the initial scaffold.

Creating the application controller

Generally, when creating an Angular application, you should define a top-level controller that uses the $rootScope service to configure some global application wide properties or methods. To create a new controller, use the following command:

```
$ yo angular:controller app
```

This command will create a new AppCtrl controller located in the app/scripts/controllers directory.

Open the app/scripts/controllers/app.coffee file and replace with the following code:

```
'use strict'

angular.module('learningYeomanCh3App')
    .controller('AppCtrl', ($rootScope, $cookieStore, Config) ->
        $rootScope.name = 'AppCtrl'
        App = angular.copy(Config)
        App.session = $cookieStore.get('App.session')
        window.App = $rootScope.App = App)
```

The preceding code does the following:

- It creates a new `AppCtrl` controller with dependencies on the `$rootScope`, `$cookieStore`, and `Config` modules

- Inside the controller definition, an `App` variable is copied from the `Config` value service

- The `session` property is set to the `App.session` cookie, if available

Creating the application views

The Angular generator will create the applications' `index.html` view, which acts as the container for the entire application. The index view is used as the shell for the other views of the application; the router handles mapping URLs to views, which then get injected to the element that declares the `ng-view` directive.

Modifying the application's index.html

Let's modify the default view that was created by the generator. Open the `app/index.html` file, and add the content right below the following HTML comment:

```
<!-- Add your site or application content here -->
```

The structure of the application will consist of an article element that contains a header, section, and footer. Replace with the following content:

```
<article id="app" ng-controller="AppCtrl" class="container">
  <header id="header" ng-include="App.layout.header"></header>
  <section id="content" class="view-animate-container">
    <div class="view-animate" ng-view=""></div>
  </section>
  <footer id="footer" ng-include="App.layout.footer"></footer>
</article>
```

In the preceding code:

- The `article` element declares the `ng-controller` directive to the `AppCtrl` controller

- The `header` element uses an `ng-include` directive that specifies what template to load, in this case, the header property on the `App.layout` object

- The `div` element has the `view-animate-container` class that will allow the use of CSS transitions

- The `ng-view` attribute directive will inject the current routes view template into the content

- The `footer` element uses an `ng-include` directive to load the footer specified on the `App.layout.footer` property

 Use `ng-include` to load partials, which allows you to easily swap out templates.

Creating Angular partials

Use the `yo angular:view` command to create view partials that will be included in the application's main layout. So far, we need to create three partials that the index view (`app/index.html`) will be consuming from the `App.layout` property on the `$rootScope` service that defines the location of the templates.

 Names of view partials typically begin with an underscore (_).

Creating the application's header

The header partial will contain the site title and navigation of the application. Open a terminal and execute the following command:

```
$ yo angular:view _header
```

This command creates a new view template file in the `app/views` directory.

Open the `app/views/_header.html` file and add the following contents:

```html
<div class="header">
  <ul class="nav nav-pills pull-right">
    <li ng-repeat="item in App.menu"
      ng-class="{'active': App.location.path() === item.href}">
      <a ng-href = "#{{item.href}}"> {{item.title}} </a>
    </li>
  </ul>
  <h3 class="text-muted"> {{ App.sitetitle }} </h3>
</div>
```

The preceding code does the following:

- It uses the {{ }} data binding syntax to display App.sitetitle in a heading element
- The ng-repeat directive is used to repeat each item in the App.menu array defined on $rootScope

Creating the application's footer

The footer partial will contain the copyright message and current version of the application. Open the terminal and execute the following command:

```
$ yo angular:view _footer
```

This command creates a view template file in the app/views directory.

Open the app/views/_footer.html file and add the following markup:

```
<div class="app-footer container clearfix">
    <span class="app-sitecopy pull-left">
      {{ App.sitecopy }}
    </span>
    <span class="app-version pull-right">
      {{ App.version }}
    </span>
</div>
```

The preceding code does the following:

- It uses a div element to wrap two span elements
- The first span element contains data binding syntax referencing App.sitecopy to display the application's copyright message
- The second span element also contains data binding syntax to reference App.version to display the application's version

Customizing the main view

The Angular generator creates the main view during the initial scaffold. Open the `app/views/main.html` file and replace with the following markup:

```html
<div class="jumbotron">
  <h1>{{ App.feature.title }}</h1>
  <img ng-src="{{ App.feature.image  }}"/>
    <p class="lead">
      {{ App.feature.body }}
    </p>
</div>
<div class="marketing">
  <ul class="media-list">
      <li class="media feature" ng-repeat="item in App.features">
      <a class="pull-left" href="#">
        <img alt="{{ item.title }}"
                  src="http://placehold.it/80x80"
                  ng-src="{{ item.image }}"
           class="media-object"/>
      </a>
      <div class="media-body">
        <h4 class="media-heading">{{item.title}}</h4>
        <p>{{ item.body }}</p>
      </div>
    </li>
  </ul>
</div>
```

The preceding code does the following:

- At the top of the view, we use the {{ }} data binding syntax to display the title and body properties declared on the `App.feature` object

- Next, inside the `div.marketing` element, another `div` element is declared with the `ng-repeat` directive to loop for each item in the `App.features` property

- Then, using the {{ }} data binding syntax wrapped around the title and body properties from the item being repeated, we output the values

Previewing the application

To preview the application, execute the following command:

```
$ grunt serve
```

Your browser should open displaying something similar to the following screenshot:

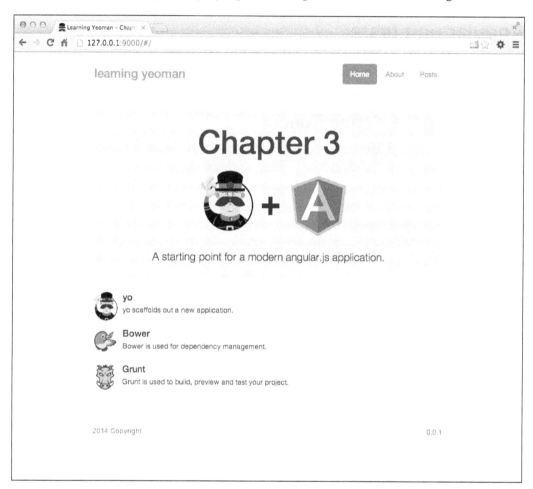

 Download the AngularJS Batarang (http://goo.gl/0b2GhK) developer tool extension for Google Chrome for debugging.

Testing an Angular application

Testing an Angular application is very easy when using Yeoman because all the configuration files are created during the initial project scaffold and all the subgenerators create a test spec that can easily be customized with specific functionality.

Angular unit tests

When scaffolding new files using the Yeoman Angular generator, the subgenerators create skeleton specs that are located in the `test/spec` directory. Yeoman makes it extremely easy to start testing your scripts.

Configuring the Karma Runner

Since the application is using various client-side dependencies, you will need to add the library locations to the `test/karma.conf.coffee` file:

```
//Line #15
files: [
  //Bower Dependencies
  'bower_components/jquery/jquery.js',
  'bower_components/bootstrap/dist/js/bootstrap.js',
  ...
],
```

Running unit tests

To run the tests for the application, execute the following command:

```
$ grunt test
```

The preceding command will do the following:

1. It will compile all projects scripts in the `app/scripts` directory to the `.tmp/scripts` directory.
2. Then, invoke the Karma that will launch Chrome and start the runner.
3. It will show the output of the tests in the console as they go.

> You can invoke the Karma runner directly by executing:
> `$ karma start test/karma.conf.coffee.`

The results from the test task should look similar to the following screenshot:

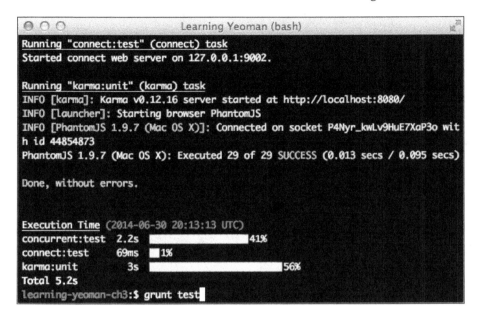

End-to-end tests with Protractor

Being able to test the functionality of the code in the application is always a good thing, but being able to run actual browser tests that mimic the actions of a real user is priceless. The folks over at Angular have created a new end-to-end testing framework that goes by the name of **Protractor**, which is built on top of the Selenium WebDriverJS.

The npm installs Protractor. To install the project, execute the fo+llowing command:

```
$ npm install -g protractor
```

This command will install the Protractor library globally, which then can be invoked from any directory. After installing it, you will need to update Selenium; Protractor includes `webdriver-manager`, which allows you to update and start the standalone server.

To download and update the Selenium Server, execute the following command:

```
$ webdriver-manager update
```

The command above will download the latest driver from Selenium and place it in the correct directory. To start the server, use the following command:

```
$ webdriver-manager start
```

This command will kick off the Selenium Server process that is run in the background, allowing you to run your Protractor tests. You should see the following screenshot if it's working correctly:

```
● ○ ○                    Learning Yeoman (node)
22:59:36.742 INFO - Default driver org.openqa.selenium.ie.InternetExplorerDriver re
gistration is skipped: registration capabilities Capabilities [{platform=WINDOWS, e
nsureCleanSession=true, browserName=internet explorer, version=}] does not match wi
th current platform: MAC
22:59:36.768 INFO - RemoteWebDriver instances should connect to: http://127.0.0.1:4
444/wd/hub
22:59:36.768 INFO - Version Jetty/5.1.x
22:59:36.769 INFO - Started HttpContext[/selenium-server/driver,/selenium-server/dr
iver]
22:59:36.769 INFO - Started HttpContext[/selenium-server,/selenium-server]
22:59:36.769 INFO - Started HttpContext[/,/]
22:59:36.794 INFO - Started org.openqa.jetty.jetty.servlet.ServletHandler@1a970e7c
22:59:36.794 INFO - Started HttpContext[/wd,/wd]
22:59:36.797 INFO - Started SocketListener on 0.0.0.0:4444
22:59:36.797 INFO - Started org.openqa.jetty.jetty.Server@1a15deb6
```

Configuring Protractor

To configure Protractor to run tests against your application, you will need to create a configuration file that contains settings for the location of test specs, the driver URL, and so on. First, create a configuration file named e2e.conf.js in the projects root directory.

Open the e2e.conf.js file and add the following content:

```
exports.config = {
  seleniumAddress: 'http://localhost:4444/wd/hub',
  capabilities: {
    'browserName': 'chrome'
  },
  specs: ['test/e2e/*.js'],
  jasmineNodeOpts: {
    showColors: true
  }
};
```

In the preceding code:

- The exports.config object holds properties that are passed to Protractor
- The seleniumAddress property specifies the location of the WebDriver server that is running

- The `capabilities` property contains the browser capabilities to enable; here we are specifying to use the Chrome browser; other options can include PhantomJS

- The `specs` property specifies the location of the test specs to run

- The `jasmineNodeOpts` property specifies what options to pass to the Jasmine node module

Creating Protractor e2e spec

Now, let's create a simple example spec that will load the application and check if the site title matches what we are expecting. Create an empty file named `app.js` in the `test/e2e` directory.

Open the `test/e2e/app.js` file and add the following content:

```
describe('Chapter3 e2e:', function() {
  beforeEach(function() {
    browser.get('http://localhost:9000');
  });
  it('should have site title', function() {
    var siteTitle;
    siteTitle = element(protractor.By.binding('App.sitetitle'));
    expect(siteTitle.getText()).toEqual('Learning Yeoman');
  });
});
```

To run the tests, just open the terminal and execute the following command:

```
$ protractor e2e.conf.js
```

This command will start the Protractor runner and execute the specs specified in the configuration file.

Angular controllers

The controllers in an Angular app are the most important things in the application. They define the scope for the view, which acts as a proxy by receiving user actions or input and performing the proper operations with the assistance of Angular services and/or custom services that third party modules expose.

Creating controllers

Creating Angular controllers is very easy using the angular:controller generator; to create a new controller, open the terminal and execute the following command:

```
$ yo angular:controller posts
```

The preceding command creates a new `PostsCtrl` controller located in the `app/scripts/controllers` directory.

Using controllers

Generally, in Angular, you use controllers to handle view-specific interactions and handle setting up the model data for the templates to display.

To demonstrate this, open the `app/scripts/controllers/posts.coffee` file and add the following code:

```coffee
'use strict'
angular.module('learningYeomanCh3App').controller 'PostsCtrl',
($scope, $location, Posts) ->
  $scope.name = 'Posts'
  $scope.posts = Posts.query()

  $scope.add = ()->
    $location.path('/posts/new')

  $scope.view = (id)->
    $location.path('/posts/view/' + id)
```

The preceding code does the following:

- It defines a controller on the `learningYeomanCh3App` module and dependencies on the `$scope`, `$location`, and `Posts` services
- The `name` property is set on the scope with the value of `Posts`
- The `posts` property is set on the scope to the value returned from the `Posts.query()` method
- The `add` function on the scope will handle sending the browser to the `/posts/new` URL
- The `view` function on the scope will handle sending the browser to the `/posts/view/:id` URL, where `id` is dynamic and comes from the view

For more information on controllers, visit
http://goo.gl/8Yk1vg.

Testing controllers

The angular:controller generator creates a controller spec file when the
angular:controller generator is invoked. The controller specs are located
in the test/specs/controllers directory.

To demonstrate testing the controller created now, open the test/specs/
controllers/posts.coffee spec and add the following code:

```
'use strict'
describe 'Controller: PostsCtrl', () ->
  beforeEach module 'learningYeomanCh3App'

  PostsCtrl = {}
  scope = {}
  location = {}

  beforeEach inject ($controller, $rootScope, $location) ->
    scope = $rootScope.$new()
    location = $location
    PostsCtrl = $controller 'PostsCtrl', {
      $scope: scope
      $location: location
    }

  it 'should have name equal to "Posts" on the scope', () ->
    expect(scope.name).toBe('Posts')

  it 'should change the location to /posts/new', () ->
    location.path('/posts')
    scope.add()
    expect(location.path()).toEqual('/posts/new')

  it 'should change the location to /posts/view/:id', () ->
    location.path('/posts')
    scope.view(1)
    expect(location.path()).toEqual('/posts/view/1')
```

In the preceding code:

- At the top, the describe method is used to contain the inner code into a spec named Controller: PostsCtrl

- The beforeEach method handles loading the module named learningYeomanCh3App for testing

- The PostsCtrl, scope, and location private variables are declared and will be set inside another beforeEach method

- The beforeEach method runs before each spec defined below; inside the beforeEach method, we use the inject method to load the proper Angular services that will be referenced by the private variables defined above

- The first it block expects that the scope.name property matches 'Posts'

- The second it block handles testing the URL location when the add() method is invoked

- The third it block handles testing the URL location when the view(id) method is invoked

Angular services

In Angular, services are singleton objects or functions that contain methods common with web applications. Angular has a number of built-in services that simplify various tasks within a web application. Angular also supports custom services that allow a developer to create reusable modules with ease.

Creating services

The angular:service subgenerator handles creating a new Angular service. Let's create a simple $resource service that will be used to connect to a RESTful backend API service; open the terminal and execute the following command:

```
$ yo angular:service Posts
```

The preceding command does the following:

- It will create a new service located in the app/scripts/services directory

- This service will use the Angular $resource service

Using services

A service is a reusable piece of business logic independent of views. Let's add the logic to handle connecting to a RESTful backend API to access; open the `app/scripts/services/posts.coffee` file and add the following content:

```
'use strict'
angular.module('learningYeomanCh3App').factory 'Post', ($resource) ->
  return $resource('/api/posts/:id', { id: '@_id' }, {
    'query': method: 'GET', isArray: true
    'update': method : 'PUT'
  })
```

The preceding code does the following:

- Defines a new factory service named `Post` on the main module with a dependency on the `$resource` service
- The factory service returns a `$resource` instance with a custom `update` method that changes the request method to `PUT`
- This factory can be used to access RESTful API services

Testing services

The angular:service subgenerator will create a service test spec located in the `test/spec/services` directory when invoked. Open the `test/spec/services/post.coffee` file and add the following code:

```
'use strict'
describe 'Service: Post', () ->

  beforeEach module 'learningYeomanCh3App'

  Post = {}
  httpBackend = null
  mockData = [{_id: 1}, {_id:2}, {_id:3}]

  beforeEach inject (_$httpBackend_, _Post_) ->
    Post = _Post_
    httpBackend = _$httpBackend_

  it 'should fetch list of posts', () ->
```

```
httpBackend.expectGET('/api/posts').respond(mockData)
posts = null
promise = Post.query().$promise
promise.then((data)->
    posts = data
)
expect(posts).toBeNull()
httpBackend.flush()
expect(posts.length).toEqual(3)
```

In the preceding code:

- At the top, the describe method is used to contain the inner code into a spec named Service: Post

- The beforeEach method handles loading the module named learningYeomanCh3App for testing

- The second beforeEach method injects the service for the spec, which is set to the local Post variable

- The it block expects that the Posts service should fetch a list of posts

- Inside the function, the httpBackend.expectGET method is used to expect a GET request to the passed argument that is the URL of the request and respond to the request with the mock data defined in the spec

- The local posts variable is set to null because the service should fulfill the promise with the returned data

- The expect method is used to ensure whether the posts variable is null before the request is made

- The httpBackend.flush() method is used to process any pending requests

- The last expect method is used to check whether the length of the posts variable matches the expected length, which is 3

 For more information on testing, visit http://goo.gl/BDo0jZ.

Angular filters

A filter formats the data for display to the user. In Angular, filters are used in expressions, which can be used in templates, controllers, or services. Angular includes several filters for formatting various types of data.

 For more information on filters, visit `http://goo.gl/Mvhe0S`.

Creating filters

The angular:filter subgenerator handles creating a new Angular filter. Let's create a `markdown` filter that will convert markdown to HTML; open the terminal and execute the following command:

```
$ yo angular:filter markdown
```

The preceding command will create a new filter located in the `app/scripts/filters` directory. This directive will use a third-party library for conversion, so execute the following command:

```
$ bower install markdown --save
```

This will download and install the markdown library in the `app/bower_components` directory.

To install this library into the `app/index.html` file, execute the following command:

```
$ grunt wiredep
```

The preceding command will attempt to wire all components listed in the project's `bower.json` file to the `app/index.html` page by adding a `script` tag referencing the `main .js` file defined in the components metadata.

 Remember to add this library to the Karma configuring file before running unit tests.

Using filters

The filter definition is simply a function that returns a string; the first argument of the function is the input value to be filtered and any arguments passed after are parameters passed to the filter function. Open the `app/scripts/filters/markdown.coffee` file and add the following content:

```
'use strict'
angular.module('learningYeomanCh3App').filter 'markdown', () ->
  (input, truncate) ->
    input = input.substring(0, truncate) if input and truncate
    return (markdown.toHTML(input)) if input
```

In the preceding code:

- It creates a new filter named `markdown` on the `learningYeomanCh3App` module

- The filter takes two arguments in the `return` function; the first argument will be converted to markdown and the second argument will be the length of the string

- Inside the function, the returned string is set to the first argument; if there is a second argument passed, then the length of the returned string is the number passed as the second argument

- The filter returns the parsed input value that is passed and returned from the `markdown.toHTML` method, if there is an input value

Testing filters

The angular:filter subgenerator will create a filter test spec located in the `test/spec/filters` directory when invoked. It is up to the developer to add the testing logic. Let's write a test for the created filter now. Open the `test/spec/filters/markdown.coffee` file and add the following code:

```
'use strict'
describe 'Filter: markdown', () ->
  markdown = {}
  beforeEach module 'learningYeomanCh3App'
  beforeEach inject ($filter) ->
    markdown = $filter 'markdown'

  it 'should return the input converted to HTML', () ->
    input = '#Heading 1'
    output = '<h1>Heading 1</h1>'
    expect(markdown(input)).toBe(output)

  it 'should return input to HTML, truncated length', () ->
```

```
input = 'This text is **bold**, and this will be truncated.'
output = '<p>This text is <strong>bold</strong>, and</p>'
expect(markdown(input, 26)).toBe(output)
```

The preceding code does the following:

- At the top, the `describe` method is used to contain the inner code into a spec named `Filter: markdown`

- The `beforeEach` method handles loading the module named `learningYeomanCh3App` for testing

- The second `beforeEach` method injects the filter for the spec, which is set to the local markdown variable

- The first `it` block tests if the passed input is converted to the expected output

- The second `it` block tests if the passed input is converted to HTML and limited to the length passed in the second argument of the filter function

 For more information, visit `http://goo.gl/M3fhsT`.

Angular directives

A directive in Angular is a reusable declarative HTML component with custom attributes and/or elements with self-contained logic that instructs Angular's HTML compiler to attach the specified behavior to that DOM element or transform the DOM element and its children.

 For more information on directives, visit `http://goo.gl/4bGGBh`.

Creating directives

The `angular:directive` subgenerator handles creating a new Angular directive. Let's create a loading directive by opening the terminal and executing the following command:

```
$ yo angular:directive loading
```

The preceding command creates a new directive located in the `app/scripts/directives` folder. This directive will handle showing or hiding the element when the route is changing.

Using directives

A directive contains reusable functionality that can be used in view templates.
Let's add the logic to the loading directive; open app/scripts/directives/
loading.coffee and add the following code:

```coffee
'use strict'
angular.module('learningYeomanCh3App').directive('loading',
  ($rootScope) ->
    template: '<p>Loading...</p>'
    restrict: 'EA'
    replace: true
    link: (scope, element, attrs) ->
      element.addClass('loading').fadeOut('fast')
      $rootScope.$on( '$routeChangeStart', ->
        element.fadeIn('fast')
      )
      $rootScope.$on('$routeChangeSuccess', ->
        element.fadeOut()
      )
)
```

The preceding code does the following:

- It defines a new loading directive on the learningYeomanCh3App module, with dependencies on the $rootScope service

- The directive definition consists of an object with properties that define how the directive is used

- The template property is set to an inline string that will simply display the text Loading...

- The restrict property is set to EA, which informs Angular how to allow only an element or attribute to use this directive

- The replace property is set to true, which informs Angular to replace the content with the content defined in the template property

- The link property is set to a function that is invoked by Angular to wire the directive

- Inside the link function, the element gets the loading class added and is hidden using the jQuery fadeOut method

- Then, the $rootScope.$on method will bind to the $locationChangeStart event dispatched by the router and show the element using the fadeIn method

- Then, the $rootScope.$on method will bind to the $locationChangeSuccess event dispatched by the router and hide the element using the fadeOut method

Testing directives

The `angular:directive` subgenerator will create a directive test spec located in the `test/spec/directives` directory when invoked. Open the `test/spec/directives/loading.coffee` file and add the following code:

```
'use strict'
describe 'Directive: loading', () ->
  beforeEach module 'learningYeomanCh3App'
  scope = {}

  beforeEach inject ($controller, $rootScope, $location) ->
    scope = $rootScope.$new()
    scope.location = $location

  it 'should replace element with Loading...', inject ($compile) ->
  element = angular.element '<loading></loading>'
  element = $compile(element) scope
  expect(element.text()).toBe 'Loading...'
```

In the preceding code:

- At the top, the `describe` method is used to contain the inner code into a spec named `Directive: loading`
- The `beforeEach` method handles loading the module named `learningYeomanCh3App` for testing
- The second `beforeEach` method injects the proper dependencies for the spec, which are set to local variables
- The `it` block defines that the directive should replace the element with the `Loading...` text
- The `$compile` method is used to compile the directive into HTML against the scope
- The `expect` method is used to check the text value of the element, which should be `Loading...`

 For more information on testing, visit `http://goo.gl/m5UaDH`.

Angular views

Creating views is extremely easy with Yeoman using the angular:view subgenerator. Let's create the CRUD views for the application.

Creating the Angular views

To create a new view, open the terminal and execute the following command:

```
$ yo angular:view [name]
```

 To create a view, controller, and route, use yo angular:route.

Creating the posts list

Let's create a view that will list all the posts defined on the scope. Open the terminal and execute the following command:

```
$ yo angular:view posts
```

The preceding command creates a new posts.html template located in the app/views directory. This view will contain angular specific directives along with custom filters to display a list of posts.

Open the app/views/posts.html file and add the following code:

```
<div id="posts">
  <button class="btn btn-default pull-right"
    ng-click="add()">Add New</button>
  <ol class="breadcrumb">
    <li><a href="#">Home</a></li>
    <li class="active">Posts</li>
  </ol>

  <ul class="posts list-unstyled">
    <li ng-repeat="post in posts | filter:tag">
      <div class="post" data-id="{{post._id}}">
        <header
            ng-include="'views/post-header.html'"></header>
        <section
            ng-bind-html="post.body | markdown:200"></section>
      </div>
    </li>
  </ul>
</div>
```

The preceding code does the following:

- It wraps the entire content in a `div` element with an ID of posts, and a simple breadcrumb list displaying the current location
- A button with the label `Add New` is declared using the `ng-click` directive that will invoke the `add()` method defined on the scope
- Then the `ul` element is declared with a class of `list-unstyled` to modify the default browser styles
- The inner `li` element is declared using the `ng-repeat` directive that will loop each item in the posts defined on the scope
- The `filter:tag` expression is used to inform Angular to only repeat items that match the defined filter
- The `header` element is used with the `ng-include` directive that will load the template into the content
- Then, the `section` element is used with the `ng-bind-html` directive set to the value of the `post.body` property
- The `markdown:200` expression will invoke the custom markdown filter to transform markdown to HTML, limited to 250 characters

Creating the post-header view

Now, we need to create a post-header view that is present in the `posts.html` view; open the terminal and execute the following command:

```
$ yo angular:view post-header
```

The preceding command does the following:

- Creates a new `post-header.html` template located in the `app/views` directory
- This view will contain elements that will be used in the list and detail views

Open the `app/views/post-header.html` file and add the following code:

```html
<div class="header">
  <a href="" ng-click="view(post._id)">
    <h1 class="media-heading">{{post.title}}</h1>
  </a>
  <span>
    Posted on {{post.created | date:'mediumDate'}}
  </span> |
    <span ng-if="post.tags">Tags:
      <span class="label label-default tag"
        ng-repeat="t in post.tags">{{t}}</span> |
```

```
            </span>
      <a href="" ng-click="edit(post._id)">
        class="btn btn-xs btn-default edit">
        <i class="glyphicon glyphicon-pencil"></i> EDIT
      </a>
    </div>
```

The preceding code does the following:

- The `div` element is declared with a class of header that will contain the title, created date, and tags of the post being repeated
- The `ng-click` directive that is used will invoke the `view(id)` method on the scope, passing the `id` of the post being repeated
- The `ng-repeat` directive is used to loop each tag in the tags array
- The `ng-click` directive that is used will invoke the `edit(id)` method on the scope

Self-test questions

The following are questions you should be able to answer at the end of this chapter:

1. What type of data binding does Angular support and what is the syntax?
2. Which Angular method allows the creation of Angular modules?
3. What type of module would one use to create a reusable UI component?
4. Which is the default testing framework used in the Angular generator?
5. What type of module would someone use to create reusable business logic?
6. How does Angular manage its dependencies?
7. How would you add the create and detail logic to expand on what we created?

Summary

In this chapter, we learned the concepts of AngularJS and how to leverage the framework in a new or existing project. We covered using the different angular subgenerators to create a CRUD application that uses custom filters, directives, and services.

We also covered the default filters and most common services that Angular includes in the library. We wrote unit tests for the custom filters, directives, and services, as well as got an inside look at how an AngularJS application is structured using the Yeoman Angular generator.

In the next chapter, we will be using the Backbone.js generator. We will cover installing the generator, using the subgenerators to create the individual files needed for a Backbone-powered single page web application.

4
My Backbone Project

Creating a modular single-page application that is scalable has always been a daunting task. However, with the Yeoman Backbone.js generator, achieving this is a lot easier than you might think.

A JavaScript library called Backbone.js gives web applications a structure with models, collections, and views that allows easy development of JavaScript applications.

This chapter is going to cover how to use the Backbone Yeoman generator to create a modular single-page application, which can be easily extended into something more. We will use each of the Backbone subgenerators to create the pieces of the application, thus giving you an insight into how to use the Backbone generator in a real-world project today.

In this chapter, we are going to cover the following:

- Many important topics on Backbone.js such as models, collections, views, routers, and events
- How to get an optimized Backbone.js project with CoffeeScript and Require.js AMD modules, set up a testing environment with Jasmine, and serve it on a Node.js server

Anatomy of the Backbone project

The concept behind Backbone is to provide a common set of data-structuring objects (collections and models) and user interface (routes and views) primitives that are useful when creating a single-page application.

The Backbone.js concepts are as follows:

- **Model**: This is a layer of abstraction that provides access to network resources
- **Collection**: This is a way to provide methods on an ordered set of models
- **View**: This is a way to encapsulate the presentation layer into objects
- **Router**: This is a way to support navigation by responding to hash changes
- **Event**: This is emitted by model and collection corresponding to the state changes

In short, Backbone.js abstracts functionality, separates concerns, and decouples code. Backbone always works with just about any library and is most often used with Require.js to load scripts; the Handlebars templating library is used to compile and render model data, and the Jasmine testing framework to create unit tests to verify the functionality. Backbone's only hard dependency is the highly popular utility library called **Underscore.js**, which gives you access to many useful functions; the library is considered a must for any developer's tool belt.

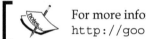 For more information on Underscore.js, visit `http://goo.gl/QRpah3`.

The new Backbone project

This new Backbone project will get you started on combining Backbone.js with **Asynchronous Module Definitions (AMD)**, using Require.js to implement a modular design and leverage Yeoman for the application structure.

Installing the generator-backbone

To install the Yeoman Backbone generator, open a terminal and execute the following command:

```
$ npm install -g generator-backbone@0.2.8
```

 The current generator-backbone version is 0.2.8.

The Backbone generator has some open issues on the Github repository; if you run into any issues, Google would be your best solution.

Scaffolding a Backbone application

To create a new Backbone project, use this two-step process; open a terminal and execute the following steps:

1. First, create a project directory named `learning-yeoman-ch4`, and make this your current directory.

2. Then, scaffold the Backbone project with Yeoman using the following command:

   ```
   $ yo backbone --coffee --test-framework=jasmine --template-
   framework=handlebars
   ```

   This command does the following:

   - It scaffolds a new Backbone application with the folder name as the application name
   - It sets the default testing framework to use Jasmine
   - It sets the default templating framework to use Handlebars

The generator will prompt for options, including those to use Twitter Bootstrap, CoffeeScript, and Require.js. The result should look similar to the following screenshot:

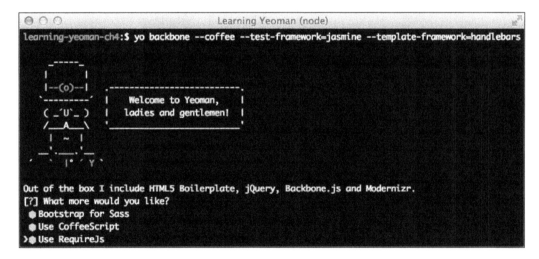

 To use Jasmine as the testing framework, generator-jasmine must be installed globally.

Understanding the directory structure

Take a moment to understand the directory structure layout of a Backbone application. The layout consists of the following:

- app: This folder contains all the frontend code, HTML, JS, CSS, images, and dependencies:
    - bower_components: This contains the client-side dependencies
    - images: This contains the images for the application
    - scripts: This contains the Backbone.js codebase and business logic
        - app.coffee: This file contains the application module's definition
        - config.coffee: This file contains the configuration module
        - main.coffee: This file contains the Require.js configuration
        - collections: This contains the application's collections
        - models: This contains the application's models
        - routes: This contains the custom filters
        - templates: This contains reusable application services
        - views: This contains the HTML templates used in the application:
            - main.coffee: This file is the main view created by default
    - styles: This contains all CSS/LESS/SASS files:
        - main.css: This is the main style sheet created by default
    - index.html: This is the application's entry point
- node_modules: This contains all project dependencies as node modules
- test: This folder contains all the tests for the application:
    - bower_components: This contains the test dependencies
    - spec: This contains unit test's mirroring structure of the app/scripts folder
    - bower.json: This file contains testing dependencies
- Gruntfile.js: This file contains all project tasks
- package.json: This file contains project information and dependencies
- bower.json: This file contains frontend dependency settings
- karma.conf.js: This file contains the Karma Runner configuration

Configuring the application

Create a configuration module that will store application properties in a separate file, which will be used when bootstrapping the application. Create a new `config.coffee` file in the `app/scripts` directory.

Open the `app/scripts/config.coffee` file and add the following content:

```coffee
define "config", [], ->
  window.Config =
    baseurl: document.location.origin
    sitetitle: "Learning Yeoman"
    sitedesc: "a starting point for a modern backbone.js app."
    sitecopy: "2014 Copyright"
    version: "0.0.1"
    email: "admin@email.com"
    debug: true
    feature:
      image: "http://goo.gl/fOq55C"
      title: "Chapter 4"
      body: "A starting point for a modern backbone.js application."
    features: [
        title: "CoffeeScript"
        body: "CoffeeScript is a little language that compiles into
          JavaScript..."
        image: "http://goo.gl/DTiliC"
      ,
        title: "BackboneJS"
        body: "Backbone.js gives structure to web applications by
          providing..."
        image: "http://goo.gl/94Pe0E"
      ,
        title: "RequireJS"
        body: "RequireJS is a JavaScript file and module loader..."
        image: "http://goo.gl/GOc6Mr"
    ]
    menu: [
        title: "Home"
        href: "/"
      ,
        title: "About"
        href: "/about"
      ,
        title: "Posts"
        href: "/posts"
    ]
```

The following actions are performed in the preceding code:

- It creates a new module using the `define` method to enclose the script
- It returns an object that has properties common to the application
- The `feature` property is an object that will be displayed in the main view that we will create
- The `features` property is an array of featured items that will be displayed in the main view as well
- The `menu` property is an array of menu items that will be displayed for the navigation of the site

Scaffolding the app view

The application will need to render upon initial loading of the browser and have a top-level view that all other views render into. Open the terminal and execute the following command:

```
$ yo backbone:view app
```

The preceding command does the following:

- It will create a new Backbone view located in the `app/scripts/views` directory
- Then, it will create a new Handlebars template located in the `app/scripts/templates` directory

The Backbone app view

The `AppView` will extend the `Backbone.View` class and perform the duties of rendering the application's layout template into the DOM. Open the `app/scripts/views/app.coffee` file and replace with the following code:

```coffee
define ['jquery', 'underscore', 'backbone', 'templates'],
  ($, _, Backbone, JST) ->
    class AppView extends Backbone.View
      template: JST['app/scripts/templates/app.hbs']
      el: '.content'
      initialize : () ->
        console.log(@)
        @render()
      render: () ->
        @$el.html(@template(@model))
        return @
```

The following actions are performed in the preceding code:

- An `AppView` class is declared by extending the `Backbone.View` class
- The `template` property is specified to the path of the Handlebars template
- The `initialize` method gets invoked when a new instance is created and will invoke its `render` method
- The `render` method is simply setting the current elements' HTML to the `template` property, passing the views model as the argument; the `template` method will take the `template` property and the object passed, and return a compiled HTML for display

The Handlebars app template

Now, let's create the template for the `AppView` class; open the `app/scripts/templates/app.hbs` file and add the following code:

```
<article id="app" class="container">
  <header id="header" class="header">
    <ul class="nav nav-pills pull-right">
      {{#each menu}}
        <li>
          <a href="#{{href}}">{{title}}</a>
        </li>
      {{/each}}
    </ul>
    <h3 class="brand text-muted">{{sitetitle}}</h3>
  </header>
  <section id="content" class="content"></section>
  <footer id="footer" class="footer">
      <span class="app-sitecopy pull-left">
          {{ sitecopy }}
      </span>
      <span class="app-version pull-right">
          {{ version }}
      </span>
  </footer>
</article>
```

The following actions are performed in the preceding code:

- An article element with the `id` attribute of the app is declared and will act as the container for the application
- A `header` element is declared with `h3` `{{sitetitle}}` for the name of the application

- Inside the `header` element, the handles `{{each}}` helper is used to repeat each item in the menu
- A `section` element is used to house the content for the different views
- A `footer` element is used to display the site copy and site version

Scaffolding the main view

The application needs a main view that will render when the index page is loaded. Open up a terminal and execute the following command:

```
$ yo backbone:view main
```

The Backbone main view

The `MainView` class will render the default view for the application. Open the `app/scripts/views/main.coffee` file replace with add the following content:

```
define ['jquery','underscore','backbone','templates'],
  ($, _, Backbone, JST) ->
  class MainView extends Backbone.View
    template: JST['app/scripts/templates/main.hbs']
    initialize: () ->
      console.log('initialize MainView', @)
    render: () ->
      @$el.html(@template(@model))
      return @
```

The following actions are performed in the preceding code:

- A new `MainView` class is created; it extends the `Backbone.View` class
- The `template` property is specified to the path of the Handlebars template
- The `initialize` method is just logging to the console for the view that is created

The `render` method is simply setting the current elements' HTML to the `template` property, passing the views model as the argument, The `template` method will take the `template` property and the object passed, and return a compiled HTML for display. As we specified Handlebars as the template framework, invoking `template()` as a function returns HTML.

The Handlebars main template

The main view needs to have some content, so add the following HTML to the `app/scripts/templates/main.hbs` file:

```
<div class="jumbotron hero-unit">
  <h1>{{ feature.title }}</h1>
  <img src="{{ feature.image}}" class="img-"/>
  <p class="lead">
    {{feature.body}}
  </p>
</div>
<div class="marketing">
  <ul class="media-list">
    {{#each features}}
      <li class="media feature">
      <a class="pull-left" href="#">
       <img alt="{{ title }}" src="{{ image }}"
             class="media-object"/>
      </a>
        <div class="media-body">
          <h4 class="media-heading">{{title}}</h4>
          <p>{{ body }}</p>
        </div>
      </li>
    {{/each}}
  </ul>
</div>
```

The following actions are performed in the preceding code:

- The `div` element is used with a `jumbotron` class for some styling
- Inside the `div` element, the feature title, image, and body from the configuration will be displayed using the {{}} Handlebars data-binding syntax
- Then, using the Handlebars {{#each}} function, we loop over each item in the array, thus displaying the title, image, and body of that item

Scaffolding the app router

The router is used to handle the various locations in an application. To create a new router, open the terminal and execute the following command:

```
$ yo backbone:router app
```

The preceding command will create a new Backbone router located in the app/scripts/routes directory.

Open the app/scripts/routers/app.coffee file and replace with the following code:

```coffee
define ['backbone', 'config', 'views/app', 'views/main'],
  (Backbone, Config, AppView, MainView) ->

  Backbone.Router.extend
    currentView: null
    routes:
      '': 'index'
    index: () ->
      console.log 'index route'
      App = new AppView(el: '.container', model: Config)
      @showView(new MainView(el: '.content', model: Config))
    showView: (view) ->
      @currentView.close() if @currentView
      @currentView = view
      @currentView.render()
      console.log('showView', @)
```

The following actions are performed in the preceding code:

- A new class named AppRouter is created that extends the Backbone.Router class.

- The routes property is set to a hash of routes and callback methods to invoke when that route is matched.

- The default route that will always be triggered on page load will invoke the index() method.

- The showView method is invoked that passes a new instance of the app and main view for display.

- The showView method handles setting the currentView in the application. This method will handle rendering a view and closing the current view to avoid memory leaks.

At the top of the `app/scripts/routes/app.coffee` file, we override the `Backbone.View` class' close method that allows the application to unbind from any events that were previously bound during the initialize method of that view; the code is as follows:

```
Backbone.View::close = ->
    @unbind()
    @remove()
    @onClose() if @onClose
```

The following actions are performed in the preceding code:

- When the `close()` method is invoked, the `unbind()` method is invoked as well

- If there is an `onClose()` method on the view, then that method will be invoked as well

Bootstrapping the app

The `app/scripts/main.coffee` file is the script that configures Require.js as well as does any application's bootstrapping. Take a look at the contents of the `app/scripts/main.coffee` file:

```
#/*global require*/
'use strict'

require.config
  shim:
    underscore:
      exports: '_'
    backbone:
      deps: [
        'underscore'
        'jquery'
      ]
      exports: 'Backbone'
    bootstrap:
      deps: ['jquery'],
      exports: 'jquery'
    handlebars:
      exports: 'Handlebars'
  paths:
```

```
    jquery: '../bower_components/jquery/jquery'
    backbone: '../bower_components/backbone/backbone'
    underscore: '../bower_components/underscore/underscore'
    bootstrap: '../bower_components/sass-bootstrap/
      dist/js/bootstrap'
    handlebars: '../bower_components/handlebars/handlebars'
    config: './config'

require [ 'backbone', 'routes/app'], (Backbone, AppRouter) ->
  window.App = new AppRouter()
  Backbone.history.start()
```

The following actions are performed in the preceding code:

- The `shim` property configures the dependencies, exports, and custom initialization for older scripts that do not use `define()`

- The `paths` property configures path mappings to module names

- The `paths` property is relative to `baseUrl` or the location of the HTML page that loads Require.js

- The `window.App` object is set to a new instance of `AppRouter`, which prepare the routes

- The `Backbone.history.start()` method simply tells Backbone to begin monitoring all hash `change` events

 For more information on Require.js, visit `http://goo.gl/SKvLVB`.

Previewing the app

To run the application locally, execute the following command:

```
$ grunt serve
```

Your browser should open up, displaying something like the following screenshot:

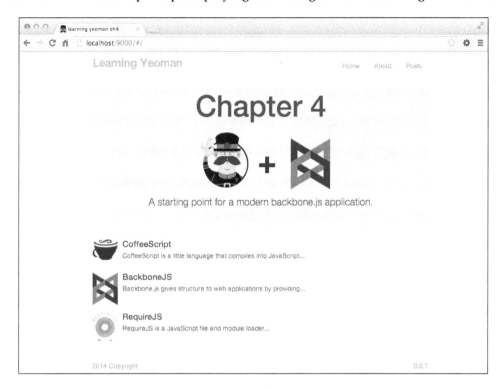

Testing

Testing the application is not as easy as 1-2-3; as we passed in the options to use CoffeeScript and Require.js, the configuration to run tests is a little bit more complex, but testing is still possible.

Configuration

First off, you will need to install the Jasmine/Require.js template; so, open a terminal and execute the following command:

```
$ npm install grunt-template-jasmine-requirejs@0.1.10 --save-dev
```

This command will download and install `grunt-template-jasmine-requirejs` into the project's `node_modules` directory and add a new entry to the `package.json` file's `devDependencies` property.

The configuration that you will need to modify is located in the `Gruntfile.js` file in the projects root directory and is around line 130 as follows:

```
jasmine: {
    all:{
        src : '.tmp/scripts/{,*/}*.js',
        options: {
            specs : ['.tmp/spec/**/*.js'],
            vendor : ['<%= yeoman.app %>/bower_components/jquery/
                jquery.js'],
            template: require('grunt-template-jasmine-requirejs'),
            templateOptions: {
                requireConfigFile: '.tmp/scripts/main.js',
                requireConfig: {
                    baseUrl: '.tmp/scripts',
                    shim: {
                        handlebars: {
                            exports: 'Handlebars'
                        }
                    },
                    paths: {
                        jquery: '../../<%= yeoman.app %>/bower_
                            components/jquery/dist/jquery',
                        backbone: '../../<%= yeoman.app %>/bower_
                            components/backbone/backbone',
                        underscore: '../../<%= yeoman.app %>/bower_
                            components/underscore/underscore',
                        handlebars: '../../<%= yeoman.app %>/bower_
                            components/handlebars/handlebars'
                    }
                }
            }
        }
    }
},
```

The following actions are performed in the preceding code:

- The `jasmine` task is modified to set the `src` directory with the compiled CoffeeScript files located in the `.tmp/scripts` directory

- The template property is set to the `grunt-template-jasmine-requirejs` node module; this module enables the Jasmine spec runner to dynamically load source and spec modules to test Require.js applications

- The `templateOptions` property is modified to reflect the locations of the required libraries by the application

- The `baseUrl` property is modified to the location of the compiled scripts to the `.tmp/scripts` location

- This configuration will allow you to test this application using the Jasmine framework with Require.js

Unit testing

Let's add an initial spec that will be used as a starting point for other tests; create a new `app.coffee` file in `test/spec`. Open the `test/spec/app.coffee` file and add the following code:

```coffee
define ['jquery', 'backbone', 'views/app', 'config'],
  ($, Backbone, App, Config) ->
   testApp = null

  describe "My Backbone Project", ->
    beforeEach(()->
      testApp = new App(model: Config)
    )
    describe 'App', ->
      it 'should have model', ->
        expect( testApp.model ).toBeDefined()
```

To run the tests for the application, use the following command:

```
$ grunt test
```

When the test task is run, you should see the console log output from the test results, which should look similar to the following screenshot:

As the generator does not scaffold the Backbone spec, adding more tests for the application is very straightforward as the configuration is taken care of.

End-to-end tests

Currently, there is no formal way of writing end-to-end scenario tests for Backbone applications. There are plenty of testing frameworks out there to choose from that will navigate your web application and perform assertions around submission of forms and more.

Here is a list of some libraries to check out:

- **Nightwatch.js**: This provides browser-automated testing with JavaScript end-to-end tests in Node.js that run against Selenium Server (http://goo.gl/Q4vvhK)

- **Casper.js**: This provides browser-navigation scripting and testing utility written in JavaScript for PhantomJS (http://goo.gl/iLYJvT)

- **Zombie.js**: This provides extremely fast, headless, full-stack testing using Node (http://goo.gl/rNeD3Z)

Backbone.Events

`Backbone.Events` is a class that can be extended into any object, allowing the object to bind and trigger custom-named events. The events can be bound at any time and can take the passed arguments.

Creating events

To use the `Backbone.Events` class, you will need to extend it into another object that will be used to trigger events or bind handlers to, for example, the following code:

```
App.pubsub = _.extend({}, Backbone.Events)
```

Using events

The easiest way to use Backbone events is to simply invoke the on or off method on any object or class in Backbone, as all classes extend from the events class, as follows:

```
App.pubsub.bind('fetch:posts', (data) ->
  alert data
)
//Usage
App.pubsub.trigger('fetch:posts', 'And send this to handler')
```

The following actions are performed in the preceding code:

- The `bind` method is invoked on the `App.pubsub` object that will bind the callback function to the event

- Using the `pubsub` object is easily done with the `trigger` method by passing the name of the event and data to be passed on to the handler

Testing events

To test events in Backbone, use a spy that will test if the event system is working, by creating events that have subscribers and making sure that the subscribers are notified when an event occurs.

Create a new `pubsub-spec.coffee` file located in `test/spec`. Open the file and add the following content:

```
describe 'App.pubsub', ->
  beforeEach ->
    pubsubSpy = jasmine.createSpy()
    App.pubsub.bind('test:event', pubsubSpy)

  it 'should trigger event handler', ->
    App.pubsub.trigger('test:event')
    expect(pubsubSpy).toHaveBeenCalled()
```

The following actions are performed in the preceding code:

- The `beforeEach` method sets up a new `pubsubSpy` event that will allow you to check the call count and so on

- The first `it` block will test if the handler is called when the event is fired

For more information on `Backbone.Events`, visit `http://goo.gl/kaF35Z`.

Backbone.Model

The `Backbone.Model` class is used to extend application-specific domain methods and logic, which provide functionality to manage changes to data, and the ability to send CRUD (GET/PUT/POST/DELETE) operations on the server and dispatch many useful events.

For more information on `Backbone.Model`, visit http://goo.gl/f9Wj21.

To bind to the model events, use the `model.on('name', callback)` function, which will trigger the callback when that event is invoked.

Scaffolding models

To create a new model, use the `backbone:model` subgenerator, open the terminal, and execute the following command to create a new post model:

$ yo backbone:model post

This command will create a new file named `post.coffee` located in the `app/scripts/models` directory; open the newly created model and add the following code:

```
define ['underscore', 'backbone'], (_, Backbone) ->
  'use strict'
  class PostModel extends Backbone.Model
    idAttribute: '_id'
    urlRoot: '/api/v2/learning-yeoman-ch3/posts'
    defaults:
      title: 'post-title'
      slug: 'post-title'
      image: 'http://placehold.it/250&text=Image'
      body: 'This is an example post with default data.'
      tags: ['featured', 'post']
      created: null
      modified: null
      published: true
    initialize: ->
      console.log('PostModel', @)
    validate: (attrs, options)->
      if attrs.title.length < 2
        return 'The title must be at least 2 characters.'
      else if attrs.title is ''
        return 'You must provide a title.'
```

The following actions are performed in the preceding code:

- The `PostModel` class is created; it extends from the `Backbone.Model` class
- The `idAttribute` property is set to the `mongodb` default id field, `_id`

- The `url` property can either be a string or a function that returns a string; in this case, it is a function that returns the endpoint URL with the id of the model appended to the URL
- The `defaults` property is set to an object, with model property keys with the default values
- The `initialize` method is used for debugging purposes to log to the console when the model is created
- The `validate` method is used to validate the `attrs` object before it is set on the model

Using the Backbone models

There are many ways to use models; you can create a new model, update an existing model, destroy a model, and validate a model and parse the response from the server before setting attributes on a model.

Creating a model

To create a new instance of a model, use the following code snippet:

```
var p = new PostModel({title: 'New Post'});
console.log( p.toJSON() );
```

The following actions are performed in the preceding code:

- The variable `p` is set to a new instance of `PostModel`
- The model is passed through a `JSON.stringify()` method and logged to the console

Updating a model

To update the properties of an existing model, use the `set()` method, as follows:

```
var p = new PostModel({title: 'New Post'});
    p.set({title: 'Updated Title'});
```

The following actions are performed in the preceding code:

- The variable `p` is set to a new instance of `PostModel`
- The `set()` method is invoked and passed with an updated attribute hash on the instance of `PostModel`
- The model is passed through a `JSON.stringify()` method and is logged to the console

Saving a model

To save a model instance on the server, use the `save()` method, as follows:

```
var p = new PostModel({title: 'New Post'});
    p.save();
```

The following actions are performed in the preceding code:

- The variable `p` is set to a new instance of `PostModel`
- The `save()` method is invoked on the model to send a POST request to the server or a PUT request if the model has an `id` attribute

Destroying a model

To destroy a model instance on the server, use the `destroy()` method, as follows:

```
var p = new PostModel({title: 'New Post'});
    p.destroy();
```

The following actions are performed in the preceding code:

- The variable `p` is set to a new instance of `PostModel`
- The `destroy()` method is invoked on the model to send a DELETE request to the server

Validating a model

To validate a model, override the `validate` method in the model definition, as follows:

```
class PostModel extends Backbone.Model
  validate: (attrs, options)->
    if attrs.title.length < 2
      return 'The title must be at least 2 characters.'
    else if attrs.title is ''
      return 'You must provide a title.'
```

The following actions are performed in the preceding code:

- The `validate` method takes two arguments: the attributes and options
- The attributes object contains the properties defined in the model
- If a model does not meet the criteria, it will return the error, and if it is valid, it returns nothing

Testing a model

To test a model, you will want to test if the model can be created with attributes, without attributes, and anything else, as follows:

```
define(['models/post'],(PostModel) ->
 describe 'PostModel:', ->
   postModel = null
   beforeEach ->
     postModel = new PostModel()
   it 'should have default attribute values', ->
     expect(postModel.get('title')).toEqual('Post Title')
   it 'should set attributes', ->
     postModel = new PostModel(title: 'NewPost')
)
```

The following actions are performed in the preceding code:

- The `define` method loads the post model module located in the `models` directory

- The `describe` method is the test suite for `PostModel`

- The `beforeEach` method simply creates a new model instance before each spec

- The `it` method is an example test case that will check to see if the model has default values

- Each of the `expect` methods simply check to see if the attribute on the model is as expected

Backbone.Collection

The `Backbone.Collection` class is used to store an ordered set of models; you can bind to collection events and fetch data from the server with RESTful routes and also include a full suite of Underscore.js methods.

 For more information on `Backbone.Collection`, visit `http://goo.gl/1JvDE1`.

Creating collections

To create a new collection, use the `backbone:collection` subgenerator as follows:

```
$ yo backbone:collection posts
```

In the preceding command:

- The `backbone:collection` subgenerator is invoked with the name of the collection set to `posts`
- The subgenerator then creates a new file located in the `app/scripts/collections` directory

As collections are ordered sets of models, the collection should have the `model` property set to a model that the collection is of; this collection is going to contain a set of post models.

Open the `app/scripts/collections/posts.coffee` file and add the following content:

```
define ['underscore', 'backbone', 'models/post'],
  (_, Backbone, PostModel) ->
    class PostsCollection extends Backbone.Collection
        model: PostModel
        url: ->
            'http://jonniespratley.me:8181/api/v2/learning-
              yeoman/posts'
        parse : (response) ->
            @trigger('posts:fetch:complete')
            return response
```

The following actions are performed in the preceding code:

- The `define` block is used to import the dependencies for this module
- The `PostsCollection` class is declared; it extends the `Backbone.Collection` class
- The `model` property is set to the model that will be contained in the collection
- The `url` property is set to a simple REST JSONP server
- The `parse` method is triggered on the response from the server by passing `response` as the parameter
- The `trigger` method is used to dispatch the `posts:fetch:complete` event

Using collections

To use the collections, just attach event handlers to a collection instance or invoke methods on a collection instance. Any event that is triggered on a model in a collection will also be triggered on the collection directly. This allows you to listen for changes to specific attributes in any model in a collection.

```
@collection = new PostsCollection()
@collection.fetch(dataType: 'jsonp')
@collection.bind('posts:fetch:complete', @render, @)
```

The following actions are performed in the preceding code:

- A new instance of `PostsCollection` is created
- The `fetch` method on the collection is invoked to request data
- When the `posts:fetch:complete` event fires, the `render` method is invoked

Testing collections

When testing collections, generally, you should test if a model can be added to the collection either as an object or an array of objects, as follows:

```
define(['collections/posts'],(PostsCollection) ->
  postsCollection = null
  describe 'Post Collection:', ->
    beforeEach ->
      spyOn($, "ajax").andCallFake (options) ->
        options.success()
      postsCollection = new PostsCollection()
    it 'should add model as object to the collection', ->
      expect(postsCollection.length).toBe(0)
      postsCollection.add({title: 'New Post'})
      expect(postsCollection.length).toBe(1)
    it 'should add models as an array to the collection', ->
      expect(postsCollection.length).toBe(0)
      postsCollection.add([
        {title: 'New Post 1'},
        {title: 'New Post 2'}
      ])
      expect(postsCollection.length).toBe(2)
    it 'should send a GET request to correct URL', ->
      postsCollection.fetch()
      request = $.ajax.mostRecentCall.args[0]
      expect(request.type).toEqual('GET')
)
```

The following actions are performed in the preceding code:

- The `describe` method wraps the inner content in a test suite
- Then, the `beforeEach` method is used to create a new collection instance and a Jasmine spy that will trigger the success method on the AJAX request
- The first `it` spec is used to test if an object can be added to the collection
- The second `it` spec is used to test if an array of objects can be added to the collection
- The third `it` spec is used to check whether an HTTP request has the correct type

The Backbone view

Backbone views are used to reflect data; they are used to listen to events and respond accordingly. The idea is to organize the user interfaces into logical views that have methods to handle user interaction and can update the UI independently when the model data changes, without having to refresh the page.

Creating views

To create a new view, use the `backbone:view` subgenerator as follows:

```
$ yo backbone:view posts
```

The preceding command creates a new Backbone view located at `app/scripts/views/posts.coffee` and a new Handlebars view template located at `app/scripts/templates/posts.hbs`.

Using views

Backbone views use an optional `render()` method that defines the logic to render a template. This example uses the Handlebars templating library to compile a collection with HTML that gets injected into the view's `el` property.

Open the `app/scripts/views/posts.coffee` file and add the following code:

```
define [
  'jquery',
  'underscore',
  'backbone',
  'templates',
  'collections/posts',
```

```
      'views/post'
], ($, _, Backbone, JST, PostsCollection, PostView) ->

    class PostsView extends Backbone.View
        template: JST['app/scripts/templates/posts.hbs']
        el: '.content'
        initialize: () ->
            _.bindAll(@, "render")
            @collection = new PostsCollection()
            @collection.fetch(dataType: 'jsonp')
            @collection.bind('posts:fetch:complete', @render, @)
            @childViews = []
            @listenTo(@collection, 'add', @renderOne)
            @listenTo(@collection, 'reset', @renderAll)

        render: () ->
            #@$el.html(@template(@model.toJSON()))
            @$el.html(@template())
            return @

        renderOne: (item) ->

            #Create new list item view passing in a single model
            itemView = new PostView(model: item)

            #Store reference to view by adding to child-views
            @childViews.push(itemView)

    #Append item to view element by the render method.
            @$el.find('.list-group').append(itemView.render())

            renderAll: () ->
            @collection.each(@renderOne, @)
```

The following actions are performed in the preceding code:

- At the top, the `define` block specifies the required dependencies that will be loaded before the script is executed

- A `PostsView` class is defined; it extends the `Backbone.View` class

- The `template` property is set to the corresponding precompiled Handlebars template

- The `el` property specifies which element to attach the view instance to

- The `initialize` method is invoked whenever a new instance of this view is created; here, we use Underscore.js' `bindAll` method to `render`, to control the scope on the view instance

- The `views` collection property is set to a new instance of `PostsCollection` and then issued to fetch data from the server by passing in `dataType` set to `jsonp`

- The `bind` method on the collection is used to invoke the `render` method when this event occurs

- The view's `childViews` property is set to an empty array that will hold the instances of all `PostView` properties that are created

- The `render` method will set the elements' content to the template and return an instance of the view

- The `renderOne` method is used to render a single model along with a single view into the content

- The `renderAll` method will loop each model in the collection and invoke the `renderOne` method

Testing views

To test Backbone views, you will want to test the initial setup, view rendering, and templating. Testing if event callbacks are triggered when the elements' action is invoked will also help ensure that the view is responding correctly to user events, as follows:

```
describe 'AppView', ->
  beforeEach ->
    sandbox = $('<div class="content"></div>')
    $('body').append(sandbox)
    testApp = new App(model: Config).render()
  afterEach ->
    sandbox.remove()
  it 'should have a header, content, and footer element', ->
      expect(testApp.$el.find('header').length).toBe(1)
```

The following actions are performed in the preceding code:

- The `describe` block wraps the inner content in a test suite

- Then, the `beforeEach` method is used to add a sandbox element to the body

- Then, a new instance of the view is created and injected into the sandbox element

- The `afterEach` method is used to remove the view from the sandbox element after every test
- The first `it` block will test if the view is rendered and has the proper child elements

For more information on `Backbone.View`, visit `http://goo.gl/KVu2Rw`.

Backbone.Router

Single-page web applications usually need to provide linkable and user-friendly links. Until recently, the only way around this was using hash fragments (/#/posts), but with the HTML5 history API, the use of standard URLs (/posts) is available. The `Backbone.Router` class provides useful methods for client-side routing in a single-page web application.

Creating routers

To create a new router, use the `backbone:router` subgenerator as follows:

```
$ yo backbone:router posts
```

This command creates a new Backbone router located at `app/scripts/routes/posts.coffee`.

Using routers

To use the `Backbone.Router` class, simply extend the class and provide the `routes` property with an object hash set on the name/callback of the route, as follows:

```
define [
  'backbone'
  'config'
  'views/app'
  'views/main'
  'views/about'
  'views/posts'
  'models/post'
  ], (Backbone, Config, AppView, MainView, AboutView, PostsView,
    PostModel) ->

  class AppRouter extends Backbone.Router
```

```
currentView: null
childViews: {}
routes:
    '': 'index'
    'about': 'about'
    'posts': 'posts'
index: () ->
  console.log('#/index route')
  App = new AppView(el: '.container', model: Config)
  @showView(new MainView(el: '.content', model: Config))

posts: () ->
  console.log('posts view')
  @showView(new PostsView(el: '.content'))

showView: (view) ->
  @currentView.close() if @currentView
    @currentView = view
  @currentView.render()
  console.log('showView', @)
```

The following actions are performed in the preceding code:

- The `define` block is used to declare all the dependencies that this module will use; in this case, all the views will be imported

- The `routes` property is set to a hash of route name and functions to invoke when the route matches

Testing routers

To test the routers, you will want to create a spy that monitors if the route's callback function is invoked when the route matches the name, as follows:

```
define(['jquery', 'backbone', 'underscore', 'routes/app'],
  ($, Backbone, _, AppRouter) ->
  router = null
  routerSpy = null
  describe "AppRouter:", ->

    beforeEach ->
      router = new AppRouter()
```

```
    routerSpy = jasmine.createSpy()

    try
      Backbone.history.start(slient: true, pushState: false)
      router.navigate('_SpecRunner.html')
    catch error
      console.log error

  afterEach ->
    router.navigate('_SpecRunner.html')

  it "should have the right amount of routes", ->
    expect(_.size(router.routes)).toEqual 6

  it 'should handle index route', ->
    router.bind('route:index', routerSpy)
    router.navigate('', true)
    expect(routerSpy.wasCalled).toBe(true)

  it 'should handle posts route', ->
    router.bind('route:posts', routerSpy)
    router.navigate('#posts', true)
    expect(routerSpy.wasCalled).toBe(true)

  it 'should not handle unknown', ->
    router.bind('route:route-doesnt-exist', routerSpy)
    router.navigate('#route-doesnt-exist', true)
    expect(routerSpy.wasCalled).toBe(false)

)
```

The following actions are performed in the preceding code:

- The `describe` block wraps the inner content in a test suite
- Then, the `beforeEach` method creates a new router instance along with a Jasmine spy
- The `Backbone.history.start` method is called to inform Backbone to start listening for route changes
- The `afterEach` method is used to reset the router's location to the default state
- The `it` block expects that the number of routes match the expectations
- The next `it` block tests that, when navigating to a different route, the callback function is invoked

For more information on `Backbone.Router`, visit `http://goo.gl/5L8zNx`.

Self-test questions

The following are the questions you should be able to answer at the end of this chapter:

1. Which library(s) does Backbone.js heavily depend on?
2. Which class do all Backbone classes extend?
3. Which option is only available in the Yeoman Backbone generator?
4. What functionality does the `Backbone.Model` class provide?
5. What functionality does the `Backbone.Collection` class provide?

Summary

In this chapter, we covered many important topics of Backbone.js such as models, collections, views, routers, and events. We also covered interesting topics on the basic project setup to get an optimized Backbone.js project with CoffeeScript and Require.js AMD modules, set up a testing environment with Jasmine, and serve it on a Node.js server.

In the next chapter, we will be using the Ember.js generator to create a single-page web application that will leverage some of the core features in the framework.

5
My Ember Project

This chapter is going to cover using the Ember.js generator to create a modern web application that can be easily extended into something more. We will use the subgenerators to create the pieces of the application. You will get a feel of how an Ember application is structured and the concepts of Ember.

In this chapter, we are going to cover the following topics:

- Creating Ember.js applications easily by using Yeoman generators
- Creating a configuration object that will hold settings for the entire application
- Exploring the Handlebars templating system by binding data from the applications' configuration file to display a list of features
- Core concepts of the Ember.js framework

Anatomy of the Ember project

The concept behind Ember is to provide developers with the tools to ambitiously build large JavaScript applications that can be used on any platform. Native application frameworks such as Cocoa and Smalltalk-76 have pioneered Ember ideas. Ember apps are structured around the URL of an application; like many JavaScript frameworks, this is not at the top of their concerns, but Ember derives the tools and concepts of its framework from the Web's most powerful thing, the URL.

The following are some Ember concepts:

- **Template**: A template is written using the Handlebars templating language and describes the user interface of the application
- **Router**: A router is used to translate a URL into a series of nested templates, each with a model that is always in sync with the current URL

- **Component**: A component is a reusable custom HTML tag that is described with a Handlebars template and JavaScript functionality
- **Model**: A model is an object that stores a persisted state; templates use models to display data to the user
- **Controller**: A controller is an object that stores an application state; templates can use controllers and/or models to retrieve properties

The new Ember project

We are going to use the Yeoman Ember generator to scaffold the pieces of an Ember. js web application. This project will get you started with a basic application that can be used as a starting point for creating a more robust application.

Installing the generator-ember

To install the Yeoman Ember generator, execute the following command:

```
$ npm install  -g generator-ember
```

The version required for the following steps is 0.8.3.

The –g flag requires an administrator user.

Scaffolding the application

First, create a folder named `learning-yeoman-ch5` and then make that your current working directory. Now, to scaffold the application, open a terminal and execute the following command:

```
$ yo ember --test-framework=jasmine --coffee --karma
```

This command does the following:

- Creates an initial project located in the current directory
- Sets the test framework to use Jasmine
- Sets the project scripting language to CoffeeScript
- Sets the project to use the Karma test runner
- And will prompt whether to use Bootstrap SASS (select Yes)

The output from the command should look similar to the following screenshot:

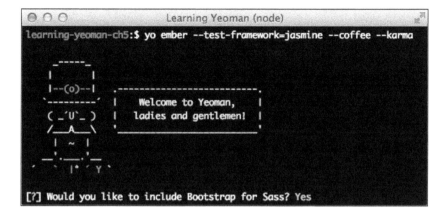

Now you are ready to start development on a fresh Ember web application.

 SASS option requires the Compass gem to be installed.

Understanding the directory structure

Take a minute to become familiar with the directory structure of an Ember application.

- app: This is where the application source code is present:
    - images: This is where images for your application go
    - scripts: This is where the application logic scripts go:
        - controllers: This is for controllers
        - models: This is for models
        - routes: This is for routes
        - views: This is for views
        - app.coffee: This is the main Ember.js app file
        - router.coffee: This is the main application router
        - store.coffee: This is the application's data store adapter
    - styles: This is for stylesheets

- ° templates: This is for Handlebar templates:
    - ° application.hbs: This is the main app template
    - ° index.hbs: This is the app index template
- ° bower_components: This contains client-side Bower dependencies
- ° index.html: This contains the application's entry point

Application configuration

Let's now go ahead and create a configuration object module that will allow us to store some application-wide properties in a separate file. Create a new config.coffee file located in the app/scripts directory.

Then, add some properties to the file that we will use when initializing the application. Open the app/scripts/config.coffee file and add the following code:

```coffee
window.Config =
  baseurl: document.location.origin
  sitetitle: 'Learning Yeoman'
  sitedesc: 'a starting point for a modern ember.js application.'
  sitecopy: '2014 Copyright'
  version: '0.0.1'
  email: "admin@email.com"
  debug: true
  feature:
    image: 'http://goo.gl/ur9Ueu'
    title: 'Chapter 5'
    body: 'A starting point for a modern ember.js application.'

  features: [
    title: 'Yeoman'
    body: 'Yeoman is a robust client-side stack.'
    image: 'http://goo.gl/W3ZtMx'
  ,
    title: 'EmberJS'
    body: 'Ember.js is built for productivity.'
    image: 'http://goo.gl/8bRsMq'
  ,
    title: 'Grunt'
    body: 'The Grunt ecosystem is growing every day.'
    image: 'http://goo.gl/xvqzS6'
  ]
  session:
```

```
    authorized: false
    user: null
  menu: [
    title: 'Home', href:'#/'
  ,
    title: 'About', href:'#/about'
  ,
    title: 'Posts', href:'#/posts'
  ]
```

The preceding code does the following:

- We declare a Config object on the window object with some application-specific properties
- The site title, site description, and site copyright are defined with defaults
- The version, email, and debug properties are declared and set
- The feature property is set to an object with title, image, and body for displaying on the index page
- The features property is set to an array with objects that contain title, image, and body properties to display on the index page
- The session property is set to an object with authorized and user properties that are currently not used
- The menu property is set to an array of objects containing title, icon, and href properties for the navigation

Application definition

The application module will have a set of commonly used properties and methods that other components can access through the global App namespace, which is set on the window object.

Open the app/scripts/app.coffee file and add the following highlighted contents:

```
require 'scripts/config'

LearningYeomanCh5 = window.LearningYeomanCh5 =
  Ember.Application.create(
  LOG_VIEW_LOOKUPS: true
  LOG_ACTIVE_GENERATION: true
  LOG_BINDINGS: true
```

```
config: window.Config
)

require 'scripts/controllers/*'
require 'scripts/store'
require 'scripts/models/*'
require 'scripts/routes/*'
require 'scripts/views/*'
require 'scripts/router'
```

The `grunt-neuter` task will concatenate files in the order you require.

The preceding code does the following:

- Before the application definition, the configuration file is required
- Then, the Ember.js application is defined with some debugging properties
- The `config` property is set to the `window.Config` object; this property is now globally accessible
- Then, we use the `require` method to load the files in order to start with the controllers and end with the router

For more information on debugging Ember, visit `http://goo.gl/GfcSzh`.

The application template

Let's go ahead and adjust the applications' default layout template. Open the `app/templates/application.hbs` file and replace the contents with the following code:

```
<article class="container">
  <header class="header">
    <ul class="nav nav-pills pull-right">
      {{#each LearningYeomanCh5.config.menu}}
      <li>
        <a {{bind-attr href=href}}>{{ title }}</a>
      </li>
      {{/each}}
    </ul>
    <h3 class="brand text-muted"> {{
      LearningYeomanCh5.config.sitetitle }} </h3>
```

```
      <hr />
    </header>
    <section class="">
      {{outlet}}
    </section>
    <footer class="footer">
      <p class="pull-left">
        {{ LearningYeomanCh5.config.sitecopy }}
      </p>
      <p class="pull-right">
        {{ LearningYeomanCh5.config.version }}
      </p>
    </footer>
  </article>
```

The preceding code does the following:

- The `article` element is declared with the `container` class; this will be the application's container
- The `header` element is declared to hold the application's navigation and title
- The `ul` element is declared with the `nag` and `nav-pills` class for styling and will contain the navigation links
- The `{{#each }}` helper is used to loop each item in the menu defined in the `config` property of the application
- The `{{bind-attr}}` helper is used to bind the value of `href` from the menu item for linking to the correct page
- The `section` element is declared to contain the output from the rendered views
- The `{{outlet}}` helper is a placeholder that the router will fill in with the proper template based on the current URL
- The `footer` element is declared to display the application's site copyright defined in the `config` property

The index template

Open the `app/templates/index.hbs` file and replace the content with the following code:

```
<div class="jumbotron">
  <h1> {{ LearningYeomanCh5.config.feature.title }} </h1>
  <img {{ bind-attr src=
    LearningYeomanCh5.config.feature.image }}/>
  <p class="lead">
```

```
      {{ LearningYeomanCh5.config.feature.body }}
  </p>
</div>
<div class="marketing">
  {{#each item in LearningYeomanCh5.config.features }}
    {{ feature-item feature=item }}
  {{/each}}
</div>
```

The preceding code does the following:

- The `.jumbtron` class is applied to a `div` element to hold the `feature` information for the application
- The `.marketing` class is applied to another `div` element that will contain the list of `feature` items
- The `{{feature-item feature=item}}` component helper is used to load the `feature-item` component and the `feature` property in the component, which is set by `item`

The feature component

`Ember.Component` is a reusable view component that is completely isolated; many properties or actions are targeted at the view object and have no access to the outer context or controllers.

The simplest way to create a component is to use the ember:component subgenerator, open the terminal, and execute the following command:

```
$ yo ember:component feature-item
```

The preceding command will do the following actions:

- It will create a new template file named `feature-item.hbs` in the `app/templates/components` directory
- It will create a new component definition file named `feature_item_component.coffee` located in the `app/scripts/components` directory

Open the `app/templates/components/feature-item.hbs` file and add the following content:

```
<div class="media feature" data-id="{{feature.id}}">
  <a class="pull-left">
    <img class="media-object"
      {{bind-attr src=feature.image}}/>
  </a>
  <div class="media-body">
    <h4 class="media-heading">{{feature.title}}</h4>
    <p>{{feature.body}}</p>
  </div>
</div>
```

The preceding code does the following:

- It declares a `div` element with `.media` and `.feature` CSS classes for styling and the `data-id` attribute set to the current items `id`
- The `img` element is using a special Ember helper that will bind the `src` attribute of the element to the `image` property of the feature
- Then, an `h4` element is used to display the title of the feature item
- Lastly, the `p` element is used to display the body of the feature

Notice how we are referencing a `feature` object's property; where does this come from? Well, the `feature` object is what is passed into the component from the outer view.

You can reuse this component anywhere in the application's view templates using the name of the component `{{feature-item feature=item}}`, which helps Ember to render the content of the component with the `feature` variable set to `item`.

Previewing the application

Now, to preview the application, run the following command:

```
$ grunt serve
```

Your default browser should open the page displaying something similar to the following screenshot:

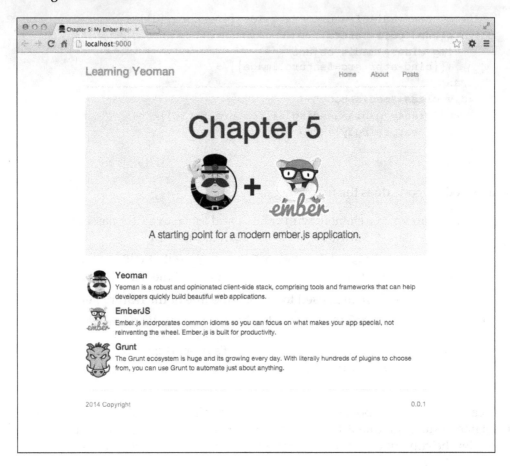

You can make changes to the code and watch the browser LiveReload automatically; thanks to the watch task, which monitors files and executes Grunt tasks.

 Try the Ember Inspector for Google Chrome at
`http://goo.gl/7ExhIj`.

Testing

Testing an Ember application is easy. Ember includes several helpers to aid with integration testing; these helpers are aware of asynchronous behavior in the application and make it extremely easy to write tests.

The test helpers

Ember provides some useful helper methods for integration testing, which are as follows:

- `visit(url)`: This visits the given route (`url`) and returns a promise that is resolved when all async behavior is complete

- `find(selector, context)`: This locates an element by `selector` within the application and/or within the context

- `fillIn(selector, text)`: This locates an input element by `selector`, fills with the given text, and returns a promise when complete

- `click(selector)`: This locates an element by `selector`, triggers the elements' `click` event, and returns a promise when complete

- `keyEvent(selector, type, keyCode)`: This simulates a key event with `keyCode` on the element found by `selector`

Setup

Ember comes with support for integration testing and unit testing. Let's configure how the application handles testing; open `test/support/initializer.coffee` and add the following highlighted code that will handle setting up everything:

```
Ember.Test.JasmineAdapter = Ember.Test.Adapter.extend(
  asyncRunning: false
  asyncStart: ->
    Ember.Test.adapter.asyncRunning = true
    waitsFor Ember.Test.adapter.asyncComplete

  asyncComplete: ->
    not Ember.Test.adapter.asyncRunning

  asyncEnd: ->
    Ember.Test.adapter.asyncRunning = false

  exception: (error) ->
    expect(Ember.inspect(error)).toBeFalsy()
)

LearningYeomanCh5.exists = (selector) ->

  !!find(selector).length

LearningYeomanCh5.text = (selector) ->

  $.trim(find(selector).text())

Ember.testing = true
```

```
Ember.Test.adapter = Ember.Test.JasmineAdapter.create()

document.write('<div id="ember-app"></div>');
LearningYeomanCh5.rootElement = "#ember-app"
LearningYeomanCh5.setupForTesting()
LearningYeomanCh5.injectTestHelpers()
```

The preceding code does the following:

- At the top of the file, a `JasmineAdapter` class is created that will contain special async methods that are implemented by the framework.

- The `exists` helper method will simply locate the element and return the length of elements.

- The `text` helper method will locate the element and return the trimmed text value.

- Then, the `document.write` method is used to create a container that will contain the application for testing.

- Next, we set the `Ember.testing` property to `true` to inform Ember that we are testing our application.

- Then, we set `Ember.Test.adapter` to the `JasmineAdapter` object that was created by extending Ember's test adapter. This enables you to write custom adapters for just about any testing framework.

- Next, the `rootElement` property is set to the ID of the test container that is added to the document.

- Then, we invoke the `setupForTesting` method on the application to initialize testing of the app.

- Next, we invoke the `injectTestHelpers` method that informs Ember to set the test helpers on the window scope.

 Custom adapters need to provide methods for `asyncStart` and `asyncEnd` to handle asynchronous testing.

End-to-end integration tests

End-to-end integration testing is pretty straightforward with Ember; basically, when you want to assert that the application is functioning properly, displaying the correct content, and handling the correct actions, you write an integration test.

Let's write a simple integration test that will make sure the application is displaying the proper content in the application; open the `test/integration/index.coffee` file and replace with the following code:

```
describe "LearningYeomanCh5 Application", ->
  it 'should display site title, nav and site copyright', ->
    visit('/').then ->
      expect(LearningYeomanCh5.text('.brand')).
        toBe(LearningYeomanCh5.config.sitetitle)
      expect(LearningYeomanCh5.text('footer .pull-
        left')).toBe(LearningYeomanCh5.config.sitecopy)
      expect(find('.nav li').length).
        toEqual(LearningYeomanCh5.config.menu.length)

  it "should display title, image, body, and list features", ->
    visit('/').then ->
      expect(LearningYeomanCh5.text('.jumbotron
        h1')).toBe(LearningYeomanCh5.config.feature.title)
      expect(LearningYeomanCh5.text('.jumbotron
        p')).toBe(LearningYeomanCh5.config.feature.body)
      expect(find('.jumbotron img').attr('src')).
        toBe(LearningYeomanCh5.config.feature.image)
      expect(find('.feature').length).toBe(3)
```

The preceding code does the following:

- The `describe` method creates an **Index route** spec that will contain the assertion methods
- The first `it` method creates a new spec that will check for the site title, navigation, and copyright
- The `visit` method loads the index route and when complete, proceeds to run the assertions contained
- The `expect` methods will ensure that the located elements' text matches the expected value
- The second `it` method creates a new spec that will check for the feature title, image, body, and features
- The `visit` method loads the index route and when complete, proceeds to run the assertions contained
- The second `expect` methods will ensure that the located elements' text matches the expected value

- The third `expect` method will locate the element by selector, get the `src` attribute, and match it against the expected value
- The fourth `expect` method will locate the element by selector and match the length against the expected length

Unit tests

Setting up unit tests is fairly straightforward, and since the `--test-framework` flag was set to Jasmine, you can use all the Jasmine methods when writing unit test specs. For example, create a new `test/spec/app.coffee` file and add the following content:

```
describe 'PostModel', ->
    postModel = LearningYeomanCh5.Post
    it 'title should be a string', ->
        expect(postModel.metaForProperty('title').type).
          toEqual('string')
```

The preceding code does the following:

- The `describe` method creates a `PostModel` spec that will contain methods for testing the model
- The `postModel` variable is set to the `Post` model defined on the apps namespace
- The `it` method specs out the test and expects the post model's title type to be a string

To run the applications tests, open the terminal and execute the following command:

```
$ grunt test
```

The output from the preceding command should look similar to the following screenshot:

```
● ● ●                    Learning Yeoman (bash)
Running "karma:unit" (karma) task
INFO [karma]: Karma v0.12.19 server started at http://localhost:9876/
INFO [launcher]: Starting browser Chrome
INFO [Chrome 37.0.2062 (Mac OS X 10.9.3)]: Connected on socket p8mvP1ulisAiRxkOIJ_p wi
th id 84491536
Chrome 37.0.2062 (Mac OS X 10.9.3) DEBUG: 'DEBUG: --------------------------------'

Chrome 37.0.2062 (Mac OS X 10.9.3) DEBUG: 'DEBUG: Ember      : 1.5.0'

Chrome 37.0.2062 (Mac OS X 10.9.3) DEBUG: 'DEBUG: Ember Data : 1.0.0-beta.7+canary.b45
e23ba'

Chrome 37.0.2062 (Mac OS X 10.9.3) DEBUG: 'DEBUG: Handlebars : 1.2.1'

Chrome 37.0.2062 (Mac OS X 10.9.3) DEBUG: 'DEBUG: jQuery     : 2.1.0'

Chrome 37.0.2062 (Mac OS X 10.9.3) DEBUG: 'DEBUG: --------------------------------'

DEBUG: 'DEBUG: For more advanced debugging, install the Ember Inspector from https://c
hrome.google.com/webstore/detail/ember-inspector/bmdblncegkenkacieihfhpjfppoconhi'
Chrome 37.0.2062 (Mac OS X 10.9.3): Executed 3 of 3 SUCCESS (0.107 secs / 0.104 secs)

Done, without errors.
learning-yeoman-ch5:$ ▋
```

 For more information on Karma, visit http://goo.gl/gPdJi3.

Ember Data

Ember Data is a library that integrates with Ember.js to make handling data from a server seamless; it can cache locally for performance, send data to the server, and create new records on the client. Ember Data gives the user the ability to create CRUD type applications fairly quickly; using the proper naming conventions, most of the controllers and files are created at runtime to allow applications to be adaptable.

Without any configuration, Ember Data can load and save records and their relationships via a RESTful JSON API, as long as the API follows RESTful conventions. Ember Data can also be configured to integrate with existing JSON APIs that do not follow the conventions. Ember Data can be configured to handle any data your server returns.

Ember Data concepts

There are some concepts of Ember Data that should be understood in order to properly leverage all the power the module has to offer. These concepts are as follows:

- **Store**: The store acts as the central repository of all records in the application
- **Model**: A model is a class that defines properties and behavior of the data
- **Record**: A record is an instance of a model and contains data loaded from the server
- **Adapter**: An adapter is an object that handles translating requests and responses from the server
- **Serializer**: The serializer is responsible for converting raw JSON sent from the server into record objects

Models

Models in an Ember application are associated with every route. Models are set up with data by either a route implementing the `model` property in a v view using the `{{link-to}}` helper, passing the model as an argument, or invoking a route's `transitionTo` method, passing the model as its argument.

Creating a model

To create a new model, use the `ember:model` subgenerator as follows:

```
$ yo ember:model Post title:string body:string image:string
slug:string--coffee
```

The preceding command creates a new Ember model located at `app/scripts/models/post_model.coffee`.

By passing the name of the model and default attributes as `property:type`, they will be added to the model definition.

Methods

Models in Ember extend the `Ember.Object` class and are defined as `DS.Model`; there are many methods available for this class, but let's take a look at the most frequently used methods.

The following are the `DS.Model` methods:

- `changedAttributes`: This will return the object with keys of changed properties and values of the `[old, new]` array

- `deleteRecord`: This will mark the record for deletion, invoke `save()` to send to server, or `rollback()` to revert

- `destroyRecord`: This will delete the record immediately and send to the server

- `save`: This will save the record, return a promise, and send it to the external source via the adapter

- `serialize`: This will return the JSON representation of the object using the adapter's serialization

- `toJSON`: This will return the JSON representation of a record

 For more information on Models, visit `http://goo.gl/PCEGrC`.

Attributes

Models in Ember use attributes to define the properties on the model when parsing the JSON payload sent to and from the server. Attributes are defined using the `DS.attr()` method by passing the first argument as either `string`, `number`, `boolean`, or `date`, and the second argument as an object of options such as `defaultValue` or defined as the computed properties, which is a function that returns the value.

Models can also define relationships with other models by using either the `DS.belongsTo` or `DS.hasMany` method by passing in the name of the model as the argument.

For example, open `app/scripts/models/post_model.coffee` and add the following highlighted code:

```
#global Ember
LearningYeomanCh5.Post = DS.Model.extend(
  title: DS.attr('string', {defaultValue: 'Post title'})
  body: DS.attr('string')
  image: DS.attr('string')
  published: DS.attr('boolean', {defaultValue: true})
  created: DS.attr('date', {defaultValue: () -> new Date()})
  slug: (->
    @get('title').replace(/\W/g, '-').toLowerCase()
  ).property('title')
)
```

The preceding code does the following:

- At the top, the `DS.Model.extend` method is used to create a new `Post` model on the app's namespace
- The object passed to the `extend` method will set the default attributes on the model
- Three of the four types of attributes are used to define the `title`, `image`, `body`, `published`, and `slug` properties
- The `slug` property is a computed function that will take the `title`, strip all non-characters, and make it lowercase

 Slug is a part of a URL that identifies a page using human-readable keywords.

Fixtures

Fixtures in Ember allow you to define default static data that can be used when waiting for an API to become available. By changing the `ApplicationAdapter` property on the `Ember.Application` instance, you can easily change how your app communicates with a data source. Open the `app/scripts/store.coffee` file and change its load fixture data by using the `DS.FixtureAdapter` property as follows:

```
LearningYeomanCh5.ApplicationAdapter = DS.FixtureAdapter
LearningYeomanCh5.Store = DS.Store.extend({})
```

The preceding code sets the application's data adapter to use fixtures, and now to populate the fixture data, open `app/scripts/models/post_model.coffee` and add the following code:

```
LearningYeomanCh5.Post.FIXTURES = [
    id: 1
    title: 'Post 1'
    body: 'Lorem ipsum dolor sit amet, adipiscing elit.'
    image: '//placehold.it/225'
  ,
    id: 2
    title: 'Post 2'
    body: 'Lorem ipsum dolor sit amet, adipiscing elit.'
    image: '//placehold.it/225'
  ,
    id: 3
    title: 'Post 3'
```

```
    body: 'Lorem ipsum dolor sit amet, adipiscing elit.'
    image: '//placehold.it/225'
]
```

The preceding code sets the FIXTURES property on the Post model to an array of objects that contain default values.

Records

Ember uses a record to define an instance of a model, which contains the data loaded from a server. Records are used to find, create, delete, and update entities in the application; records are uniquely identified by two things:

- A model type
- A globally unique ID

Finding all records

To find all records of a model, invoke the find method on the store by passing the name of the model as the only argument, as follows:

```
@store.find('post');  // => [ { id: 1, title: 'Post 1', ... } ]
```

Finding a single record

To find a single record, invoke the find method on the store; the first argument is the name of the model and the second is the ID of the record, as follows:

```
@store.find('posts', 1);  // => { id: 1, title: 'Post 1', … }
```

Creating a record

To create a record, invoke the createRecord method on the store; here, the first argument is the name of the model and the second is an object of properties to create it with, as follows:

```
@store.createRecord('post', {
  title: 'New Post'
  body: 'This is a new post'
  image: '//placehold.it/225'
})
```

Deleting a record

To delete a record, invoke the `deleteRecord` method on the store, which will mark it for deletion, and then use the `save` method to send the command to the server for removal or the `rollback` method to revert the deletion, as follows:

```
@get('model').deleteRecord()
```

 For more information on records, visit `http://goo.gl/EfiyvL`.

Routes

Routes in Ember represent each of the possible states in the application and are represented by the URL. Every route in Ember has a model, which is always kept in sync with the current URL. Ember allows you to specify a different root URL instead of the domain's root by setting the `rootURL` property when creating a route, which allows applications to run in deeply nested domains.

As the application increases in size, you can set the `LOG_TRANSITIONS` property to `true` on the `Ember.Application` instance that allows all routes to be logged in the console, which is great for debugging, or seeing the autogenerated routes that Ember produces.

Creating the routes

To create a new route, use the ember:model subgenerator because it will generate all the necessary controllers, views, and routes. Open the terminal and execute the following command:

```
$ yo ember:model tag
```

This command will create the following:

- Creates a new model class located at `app/scripts/models/tag_model.coffee`
- Creates a new controller class located at `app/scripts/controllers/tags_controller.coffee`
- Creates a new edit controller class located at `app/scripts/controllers/tag_edit_controller.coffee`
- Creates a new view class located at `app/scripts/views/tags_view.coffee`

- Creates a new edit view class located at `app/scripts/views/tags_edit_view.coffee`
- Creates a new Handlebars view template located at `app/templates/tag.hbs`
- Creates a new Handlebars edit view template located at `app/templates/tag/edit.hbs`

Using routes

There are two things to keep in mind when using routes in Ember, which are as follows:

- **Resource**: This is the beginning of a route, controller, or template name
- **Route**: This is nested inside a resource and is added to the resource name separated by a dot (.)

For example, open the applications router located at `app/scripts/router.coffee`, and examine the following code:

```
LearningYeomanCh5.Router.map( ->
    @resource('posts', ->
    @resource('post', path: '/:post_id', ->
      @route('edit')
    )
    @route('create')
  )
)
```

The preceding code does the following:

- The application's route is defined by passing a function to the `map` property on the router
- A resource is declared for posts, and inside the posts resource function another resource is declared for editing a post, which sets the `path` to `/posts/:post_id` and the `route` to `edit`
- Then, the `create` route is defined to handle routing to `/posts/create` to add a new post

Posts route

The generator will create a route that will handle fetching all the records for the model in the store.

Open the `app/scripts/routes/posts_route.coffee` file and examine the content:

```
LearningYeomanCh5.PostsRoute = Ember.Route.extend(
  model: ->
    @get('store').find('post')
)
```

The preceding code does the following:

- The `PostsRoute` class is declared extending the `Ember.Route` class
- The `model` property is set to the records returned from the store's `find` method

This allows the controller and template to have access to the `model` property that contains an array of model records.

Post route

The generator will create a route that will handle setting the model found in the store.

Open the `app/scripts/routes/post_route.coffee` file and examine the following content:

```
LearningYeomanCh5.PostRoute = Ember.Route.extend(
  model: (params) ->
    @get('store').find('post', params.post_id)
)
```

The preceding code does the following:

- The `PostRoute` class is declared extending the `Ember.Route` class
- The `model` property is set to the record returned from the store's `find` method invoked with the routes `params`, which holds `post_id`

This allows the controller and template to have access to the `model` property that contains the properties from the record.

Posts edit route

The generator will create an edit route that will handle a finding record by ID for the model in the store.

Open the `app/scripts/routes/post_edit_route.coffee` file and examine the following content:

```
LearningYeomanCh5.PostEditRoute = Ember.Route.extend(
  model: (params) ->
    @get('store').find('post', @modelFor('post').id)
)
```

The preceding code does the following:

- The `PostRoute` class is declared extending the `Ember.Route` class
- The `model` property is set to the record returned from the store's `find` method invoked with the routes `param` property

> For more information on routes, visit `http://goo.gl/sKma5G`.

Templates

Ember has integrated the Handlebars semantic templating library to power your app's user interface. Handlebars allow the use of regular HTML markup along with the double mustache {{ }} expressions to display data and automatically update when the underlying data changes.

Handlebar helpers

Ember provides Handlebars helpers that can be used in your templates to render other views. Here is the list of default helpers:

- {{ `partial` }}: This renders the specified name of the template in the current view and has access to the current scope.

  The partial's name must start with an underscore (`data-template-name="_partial"` or `data-template-name="views/_partial"`).

- {{ view }}: This renders the specified view template and has access to the current model and controller.

  This helper works like the partial helper, except instead of providing a template to be rendered within the current template, you provide a view class.

- {{ render }}: This renders the view template in the current view and has access to the current model and controller, and takes the following two parameters:
  - ° The first parameter describes the context to be set up
  - ° The optional second parameter is a model, which will be passed to the controller if provided

Posts template

The generator will create a template that will display a list of all the records for the model in the store.

Open the app/templates/posts.hbs file and replace with the following content:

```
<div id="posts">
  <div class="page-header">
    <h1>Posts</h1>
  </div>
  <div class="list-group">
    {{#each model}}
      {{#link-to 'post' this classNames='list-group-item'}}
      <h4 class="list-group-item-heading">{{ title }}</h4>
      <p class="list-group-item-text">
        {{ body }}
      </p>
      {{/link-to}}
    {{/each}}
  </div>
</div>
{{outlet}}
```

The preceding code does the following:

- At the top, a div element is declared with the ID of posts
- A legend element is used to display the title of the page
- A div element with the list-group class is declared to hold all posts
- The {{#each}} helper is used to loop each item in the model
- The {{#link-to}} helper is used to link the current item to the PostRoute route's model property

- The heading element is used to wrap the title of the current item being repeated
- The paragraph element is used to wrap the body of the current item being repeated

Save the file and the browser should refresh; navigate to the /#/posts route and the display should be similar to the following screenshot:

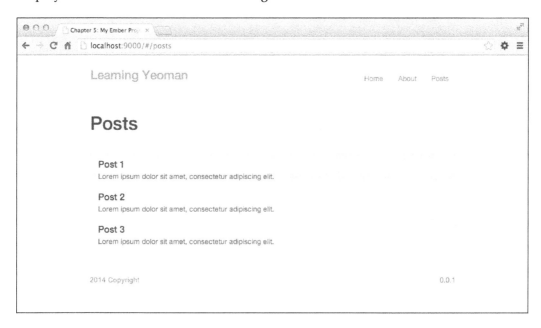

Post template

The generator will create a template that will display a detailed view of the current model in the store based on the route.

Open the app/templates/post.hbs file and add the following content:

```
<div id="post-details">
  <div class="row">
    <div class="col-md-12">
      <div class="page-header">
        {{#link-to 'post.edit' model classNames=
          'btn btn-default btn-edit pull-right'}}Edit{{/link-to}}
        <h1>{{model.title}}</h1>
      </div>
      <img class="img-thumbnail pull-right"
        {{bind-attr src=model.image}}/>
      <p>
```

```
        {{model.body}}
      </p>
    </div>
  </div>
</div>
{{outlet}}
```

The preceding code does the following:

- At the top, a `div` element is declared with an `id` of `post-details`
- Then, another `div` element is declared with the `class` set to `row`
- Another `div` is declared with the `class` of `page-header` for styling
- The `{{#link-to}}` helper is used to link the current model to the `PostsEditRoute` route's `model` property

Save the file and the browser should refresh; navigate to the `/#/posts/2` route and the display should be similar to the following screenshot:

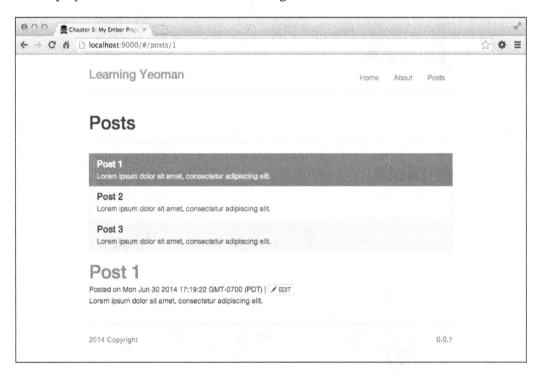

Posts edit template

The generator will create a template that will display a form view of the current model in the store based on the route.

Open the `app/templates/post/edit.hbs` file and add the following content:

```
<div id="post-edit">
  <div class="page-header">
    <h1>Edit {{title}}</h1>
  </div>
  <form role="form">
    <div class="form-group">
      <label for="title">Title</label>
      {{input type="text"  class="form-control" value=title}}
    </div>
    <div class="form-group">
      <label for="title">Slug</label>
      {{input type="text"  class="form-control" value=
        slug disabled="true"}}
    </div>
    <div class="form-group">
      <label for="image">Image</label>
      {{input type="text" class="form-control" value=image}}
    </div>
    <div class="form-group">
      <label for="body">Body</label>
      {{textarea rows="5" class="form-control" value=body}}
    </div>
    <button class="btn btn-primary" {{action 'save'}}>
      Update
    </button>
    <button class="btn btn-danger" {{action 'destroy'}}>
      Delete
    </button>
  </form>
</div>
```

The preceding code does the following:

- At the top, a `div` element is declared with an `id` of `post-edit`
- Next, a form element is declared that will contain input elements
- Then, for each property in the model, the `{{input value=property}}` helper is used to render a data binding text input

- The {{action 'save'}} action helper is used to trigger the save action defined in the PostsEditController method

- The {{action 'destroy'}} action helper is used to trigger the destroy action defined in the PostsEditController method

Save the file and the browser should refresh; navigate to the /#/posts/2/edit route and the display should be similar to the following screenshot:

 For more information on templates, visit http://goo.gl/rcmwSf.

Controllers

In Ember.js, controllers allow you to decorate your models with display logic; models have properties that are sent to the server and controllers have properties that do not need to be sent to the server.

Post edit controller

The generator will create a controller that will control the edit view; let's add some logic that will handle saving and destroying a model.

Open the `app/scripts/controllers/post_edit_controller.coffee` file and add the following content:

```
LearningYeomanCh5.PostEditController =
  Ember.ObjectController.extend(
  needs: 'post'
  actions:
    save: ->
      @get('model').save()
      @transitionToRoute 'post', @get('model')
    destroy: ->
      @get('model').deleteRecord()
      @transitionToRoute 'posts'
)
```

The preceding code does the following:

- The `PostEditController` class is defined extending the `Ember.ObjectController` class
- The `needs` property specifies that this controller depends on the `post` controller
- The `actions` object declares a `save` action and a `destroy` action
- The `save` action will get an instance of the model and invoke the `save` method, and then transitions the app to the post detail route
- The `destroy` action will get an instance of the model and invoke the `deleteRecord` method, and then transitions to the posts list route

 For more information, visit `http://goo.gl/QYFfAs`.

Self-test questions

The following are questions that you should be able to answer after reading this chapter:

1. Which template library is built into Ember?
2. Which class handles persisting data in Ember?
3. What two things uniquely identify a record object?
4. How do models define a relationship to another model?
5. How do you find a single record in Ember?
6. Which method is used to delete a model?
7. Which template helper links to a specific method on the controller, current route, or route ancestors?

Summary

We have covered how you can quickly get started with creating Ember.js applications easily by using Yeoman generators. We started off by creating a configuration object that will hold settings for the entire application. Next, we modified the application and index layouts to display the site title and navigation links, and then we explored the Handlebars templating system by binding data from the applications' configuration file to display a list of features.

We then created a simple CRUD operation that allows one to fetch records from a data store, modify them, and then save them back into the data store. We covered the core concepts of the Ember.js framework to give you an idea of how powerful and robust it truly is.

Next up, we are going to explore the world of creating custom Yeoman generators. We will take a look at using a generator to scaffold a custom generator that will be customized to scaffold a simple website using predefined templates and options.

6
Custom Generators

This chapter will cover creating custom Yeoman generators with the Yeoman generator-generator. By the end of this chapter, you will be able to create a customizable Yeoman generator that is installed using Node's package manager (npm) and made available to the community.

In this chapter, we will leverage the Yeoman API to handle processing files, install Bower components, prompt for user input, and test the generator's output using Mocha, which is a feature-rich JavaScript test framework that runs on Node.js. By the end of this chapter, you will be able to save time and money developing your next project by creating a custom Yeoman generator.

In this chapter, we are going to cover the following:

- Creating custom Yeoman generators that take multiple answers from command-line prompts and scaffold a modern web application
- Using the API to download and install libraries from Bower into the application
- Writing tests that verify the directory structure and content of files created dynamically based on user input, and publish the generator to npm for community usage
- Using the generator to create a simple test website and create custom Grunt tasks

Anatomy of a generator

Yeoman generators run in a Node.js environment and are managed by npm. They are executed from the command line, have a powerful prompting library, and leverage the Node.js API for functionality. Generators are responsible for one and only one thing—to take user input and output generated files based on that input.

Types of generators

Generally, there are two types of generators:

- **Copiers**: It simply copies boilerplate files from one location to another
- **Advanced**: It has customizable options, remote dependencies, and more

The new custom generator

We are going to create a custom generator that will scaffold a single-page web application. The project will include jQuery, Bootstrap, and Handlebars that will be managed via Bower. The project is also going to use Grunt, which will run and watch files for changes, and start a Connect LiveReload server for development.

Installing the generator-generator

First, we need to install the generator to create our generator. Open the terminal and execute the following command:

```
$ npm install -g generator-generator
```

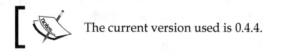 The current version used is 0.4.4.

This command will install the Yeoman `generator-generator` globally, so you can use the `yo generator` command from within any directory.

Using generator-generator

To create a new Yeoman generator, execute the following command in the directory of your generator:

```
$ yo generator
```

The preceding command will ask questions about the generator as shown in the following screenshot:

```
 ● ○ ○                    Learning Yeoman (bash)                    ⌐
learning-yeoman-ch6:$ yo generator

      _-----_
     |       |    .--------------------------.
     |--(o)--|    |   Create your own Yeoman |
     `---------'  |      generator with      |
     ( _´U`_ )    |        superpowers!      |
     /___A___\    '--------------------------'
      |  ~  |
    __'.___.'__
  ´   `  |° ´ Y `

[?] Would you mind telling me your username on GitHub? jonniespratley
[?] What's the base name of your generator? learning-yeoman-ch6
   create package.json
   create .editorconfig
   create .jshintrc
   create .travis.yml
   create README.md
   create .gitattributes
   create .gitignore
   create app/index.js
   create app/templates/editorconfig
   create app/templates/jshintrc
   create app/templates/_package.json
   create app/templates/_bower.json
   create test/test-load.js
   create test/test-creation.js
```

 Enter your Github username and a different base
generator name.

Understanding the directory structure

The directory structure that the Yeoman generator creates includes default templates and tests to streamline the creation of a new custom generator. Take a minute and review the directory structure created. The directory structure looks like the following:

- README.md: This file contains information on how to use the generator
- app: This folder contains the main module definition and templates:
    ◦ index.js: This file contains generator module definition

- ° templates: This folder contains custom boilerplate files:
  - ° editorconfig: This file contains IDE settings
  - ° jshintrc: This file contains JSHint settings
  - ° _package.json: This file contains project information
  - ° _bower.json: This file contains client-side dependencies
  - ° travis.yml: This file contains build settings for Travis CI
- node_modules: This folder contains project dependencies
- package.json: This file contains information about the project
- test: This folder contains the unit tests for the generator:
  - ° test-creation.js: This file tests the contents of the generated files
  - ° test-load.js: This file tests loading into the Node.js environment

Adding logic to the generator

The logic for the generator is located in the app/index.js file. This file defines the generator module extending from the yeoman.generators.Base class as shown in the following code:

```
'use strict';
var util = require( 'util' );
var path = require( 'path' );
var yeoman = require( 'yeoman-generator' );
var yosay = require( 'yosay' );
var chalk = require('chalk');

var LearningYeomanCh6Generator = yeoman.generators.Base.extend(..);
```

The preceding code does the following:

- The util, path, yeoman, chalk, and yosay modules are included using the require method
- The LearningYeomanCh6Generator variable declares a new generator extending from the Base class in the yeoman.genators package
- The code that gets generated inside the extend method is omitted as we will cover that later
- At the bottom of the file, the module.exports variable is set to the custom generator object that makes it available to the public

For more information on Node.js modules, visit
`http://goo.gl/TCpUR1.`

Initializing the generator

The `init` method initializes the generator by loading the `package.json` file and adding an event listener to the `end` event of the generator, as follows:

```
init: function() {
  this.pkg = require('../package.json');
  this.on('end', function() {
    if (this.options['skip-install'] !== true) {
      this.installDependencies();
    }
  });
},
```

The preceding code does the following:

- It adds an event listener on the `end` event that will install the dependencies if the `–skip-install` flag is `false` or `null`

- It sets the `pkg` property of the generator to the loaded `package.json` file in the project's root directory

Asking questions to the user

The `askFor` method asks questions to the user by displaying prompts. After the user enters the input value, the callback then loops over each property and sets the name equal to the value on the generator using the following code:

```
askFor: function() {
  var done = this.async();

  this.log(yosay('Welcome to the marvelous LearningYeomanCh6
    generator!'));
  this.prompts = [
    {
      type: 'input',
      name: 'siteTitle',
      message: 'What is the name of your site',
      "default": 'My Site'
    }, {
      type: 'input',
```

```
        name: 'siteDesc',
        message: 'What is the site description?',
        "default": 'A modern site built with a Yeoman Generator.'
      }, {
        type: 'input',
        name: 'featureTitle',
        message: 'What is the feature?',
        "default": 'Modern Site'
      }, {
        type: 'input',
        name: 'featureBody',
        message: 'The feature description?',
        "default": 'A modern site using modern tools &
          technologies.'
      }, {
        type: 'input',
        name: 'featureImage',
        message: 'The feature image?',
        "default": 'http://goo.gl/SYjnUf'
      }
    ];
    this.prompt(this.prompts, (function(props) {
      this.siteTitle = props.siteTitle;
      this.siteDesc = props.siteDesc;
      this.featureTitle = props.featureTitle;
      this.featureBody = props.featureBody;
      this.featureImage = props.featureImage;
      done();
    }).bind(this));
  },
```

Yeoman generators rely on the Inquirer.js library that handles the generators' prompts during the scaffold.

The following table lists the properties available for a question object:

Name	Type	Description
Type	Input Confirm List Rawlist	The type property specifies the types of prompts, which are input, confirm, list, and rawlist.
Name	String	The name property specifies the name to use when storing the answer in the answers hash.

Name	Type	Description
Message	String	The message property specifies the question to print.
Default	String Number Array Function	The default property specifies the value or function that returns the default value. If the type is function, the first parameter is the current session's input answer.
Choices	Array function	The choices type can be either an array of choices or a function that returns an array of string values or objects (name: value).
Validate	Function	The validate property receives the value from user input; it will return true if the value is valid, or it will return an error message if false.
Filter	Function	The filter property receives the value and returns a filtered value; the value returned will be added to the answers hash.
When	Function	The when property receives the answers hash and returns true or false depending on whether or not the question should be asked.

 For more information on Inquirer.js, visit `http://goo.gl/1Mf2ty`.

Copying the project files

The `projectFiles` method will copy all the project-specific files. Any file at a project level that needs to be included should go under the `projectFiles` method. Consider the following code:

```
projectfiles: function() {
    this.copy('_package.json', 'package.json');
    this.copy('_Gruntfile.js', 'Gruntfile.js');

    //Copy all of the bower specific files.
    this.copy('bowerrc', '.bowerrc');
    this.copy('_bower.json', 'bower.json');

    //Copy all files that handle code editing.
    this.copy('editorconfig', '.editorconfig');
    this.copy('jshintrc', '.jshintrc');

    //Copy all files that handle git repositorys
    this.copy('gitignore', '.gitignore');
```

```
    this.copy('gitattributes', '.gitattributes');

    //Copy files for Travis CI.
    this.copy('travis.yml', '.travis.yml');
},
```

The preceding code does the following:

- It will copy the files from the app/templates directory to the directory where the generator was invoked
- In this case, the package.json, Gruntfile.js, .bowerrc, bower.json, .gitignore, .gitattributes, .travis.yml, .editorconfig, and .jshintrc files will be copied from the templates directory to the root of the project

Copying the application files and folders

The app method will copy and create all the application-specific files and folders. The copy function will pass the generator instance if no third argument is set to each template; this allows you to use Underscore template expressions <%= %> to render user input in the templates, as follows:

```
app: function() {
  this.mkdir('app');
  this.mkdir('app/images');
  this.mkdir('app/scripts');
  this.mkdir('app/styles');
  this.mkdir('app/pages');
  this.copy('_index.html', 'app/index.html');
  this.copy('_main.html', 'app/pages/main.html');
  this.copy('_main.js', 'app/scripts/main.js');
  this.copy('_main.css', 'app/styles/main.css');
},
```

The preceding code does the following:

- It invokes the mkdir method that takes a string of the path where a directory should be created. Here, we create the images, scripts, and styles folders in the app directory.
- It will invoke the copy method to copy the image file from app/templates into app/images.
- Each copy method will copy the specified file in the first argument to the second argument's location, passing an instance of the generator to each file, allowing the use of Underscore templating methods inside the template files.

Installing dependencies with Bower

The `bowerInstaller` method will invoke the `bowerInstall` method that the Yeoman API provides, which will fetch the specified libraries from Bower, download them into the projects `bower_components` folder, and add the entries into the projects `bower.json` file. Consider the following code:

```
bowerInstaller: function() {
  if (this.options['skip-install'] !== true) {
    this.bowerInstall(['jquery', 'handlebars', 'bootstrap'], {
      save: true
    });
  }
});
```

The preceding code does the following:

- The `bowerInstaller` method installs the specified libraries and saves them to the `bower.json` file
- This method will only be invoked if the user did not specify the `--skip-install` flag

That wasn't so bad now, was it? We wrote six functions that extended the `yeoman.generators.Base` object that will handle the following:

- Initializing the generator and loading the `package.json` file
- Asking the session user questions and storing responses
- Copying all project-specific files into the root directory where the generator was invoked
- Creating the application-specific folder structure
- Then copying all application-specific files passing in the generator's session instance to use the dynamic values from the questions
- And finally, installing some libraries using the bowerInstall method that takes an array of dependencies to install

Now we are ready to start customizing the templates that were created by the generator-generator by default, and add some custom styles, and scripts that handle the logic for routing from page to page and loading the main view. Let's proceed to create some templates.

Creating custom templates

The generators template files are located in the app/templates directory, where the generator performs all file operations in the templates directory as the current working directory. We will create a few templates in this directory that are prefixed with an underscore (_) to indicate that the file contains Underscore.js templating syntax <%= exp %>. The files that we will create in addition to the default generated files will be the following:

- _Gruntfile.js: This file will contain the task settings
- _bower.json: This file will contain the client dependencies
- _index.html: This file will display the home page
- _main.css: This file will contain default styles
- _main.js: This file will bootstrap the app

Creating the Gruntfile.js file

The Gruntfile.js file contains the tasks for the project; there will be a task to watch files, start a development server, and wire installed Bower components to the index.html page. Create a new file in the app/templates directory named _Grunfile.js. Here is the content of the _Gruntfile.js file:

```
'use strict';
module.exports = function(grunt) {
  require('load-grunt-tasks')(grunt);
  require('time-grunt')(grunt);
  //Project tasks configuration
  grunt.initConfig({});
};
```

The preceding code defines the logic for Grunt; the module.exports function passes in the grunt instance, which allows project-specific tasks to be configured.

Creating the watch task

Now that we have the initial structure of the Gruntfile set up let's add the configuration settings for the watch task. Open the app/templates/_Gruntfile.js file and add the following watch object to the initConfig method:

```
//Watch - This task will watch files and run tasks when
  files change.
watch: {
  options: {
    nospawn: true,
```

```
      livereload: true
    },
    //Watch for index file changes and build
    livereload: {
      files: ['app/index.html', 'app/scripts/**/*.js',
        'app/styles/*.css'],
      tasks: ['build']
    },
    //Watch any bower changes and inject scripts.
    bower: {
      files: ['bower.json'],
      tasks: ['bowerInstall']
    },
  },
```

Creating the serve task

Now, let's add the configuration settings for the serve task. Open the
app/templates/_Gruntfile.js file and add the following connect
object to the initConfig method:

```
//Connect Server - The actual grunt server settings
connect: {
    options: {
        port: 9000,
        livereload: 35729,
        hostname: 'localhost'
    },
    livereload: {
        options: {
            open: true,
            base: ['.tmp', 'app']
        }
    }
},
```

The preceding code defines the server settings for the connect task. The options
task sets up the server's port, host, and livereload port. The livereload target
sets the open property to true, so the default web browser opens automatically and
the base property specifies the location of files to serve.

Creating the bowerInstall task

Lastly, let's add the configuration settings for the `bowerInstall` task. Open the `app/templates/_Gruntfile.js` file and add the following `bowerInstall` object to the `initConfig` method:

```
//Bower installer - This installs bower_component packages
  into specified files.
bowerInstall: {
    target: {
        src: ['app/**/*.html'],
        dependencies: true,
        devDependencies: false
    }
}
```

The preceding code defines the `bowerInstall target` task by setting the location of the `src` file to inject the scripts into; the `dependencies` property is set to `true`, which means that it will inject all items in the `dependencies` object in the project's `bower.json` file.

Registering tasks in Gruntfile.js

Now that we have created and configured the default tasks for the project, for the tasks to be available to the user, we will need to register a few named tasks. The tasks we will register will be a `serve` task, a `build` task, and the `default` grunt task.

Add the following to the bottom of the `_Gruntfile.js` file right before the closing bracket:

```
//Serve task - $ grunt serve
grunt.registerTask('serve', function(target) {
  console.log('running serve');
  grunt.task.run(['bowerInstall', 'build',
    'connect:livereload', 'watch']);
});

//Build task - $ grunt build
grunt.registerTask('build', 'Building the project.', function() {
  console.log('running build');
});

//Default task - $ grunt
grunt.registerTask('default', ['build', 'serve']);
```

The preceding code will register the following three tasks with Grunt:

- The `serve` task will handle starting the Connect LiveReload server that will serve the files in the `app` directory
- The `build` task will handle doing any pre-deployment tasks; feel free to customize what tasks are ran during the build phase
- The `default` task will handle running the `build` and `serve` tasks

Creating the package.json file for npm

The `_package.json` file is going to contain project-specific information that npm uses to install project dependencies. Create a new `_package.json` file in the `app/templates` directory, if it does not already exist, and then add the following contents:

```
{
    "name": "<%= _.slugify(siteTitle) %>",
    "version": "0.0.1",
    "dependencies": {},
    "devDependencies": {
        "grunt": "~0.4.1",
        "time-grunt": "~0.2.0",
        "grunt-contrib-connect": "~0.5.0",
        "grunt-contrib-watch": "~0.5.0",
        "grunt-contrib-copy": "~0.4.1",
        "grunt-bower-install": "~1.0.0",
        "load-grunt-tasks": "~0.2.0"
    },
    "engines": {
        "node": ">=0.8.0"
    }
}
```

Creating the .editorconfig file for IDEs

The `.editorconfig` file specifies the projects style guidelines for different file types; it enables developers to share a common set of formatting styles, which the project works with numerous IDEs. Create a new file in the `app/templates` directory named `editorconfig` if it doesn't exist, and add the following code:

```
root = true

[*]
indent_style = tab
```

```
indent_size = 2
end_of_line = lf
charset = utf-8
trim_trailing_whitespace = true
insert_final_newline = false

[*.md]
trim_trailing_whitespace = false
```

 For more information on EditorConfig, visit `http://goo.gl/ZpiMa9`.

Creating the .jshintrc file for JSHint

The `.jshintrc` file specifies configuration settings when JSHint is linking files in the project; it enables developers to have increased code quality by sharing a common set of coding standards. Create a new file in the `app/templates` directory named `jshintrc` if it doesn't exist, and add the following code:

```
{
  "node": true,
  "esnext": true,
  "bitwise": true,
  "camelcase": true,
  "curly": true,
  "eqeqeq": true,
  "immed": true,
  "indent": 2,
  "latedef": true,
  "newcap": true,
  "noarg": true,
  "quotmark": "single",
  "regexp": true,
  "undef": true,
  "unused": true,
  "strict": true,
  "trailing": true,
  "smarttabs": true,
  "white": true
}
```

 For more information on JSHint options, visit `http://goo.gl/ebwCEX`.

Creating the .travis.yml file for Travis CI

Travis CI is a hosted continuous integration and deployment system. There are two versions, `https://travis-ci.com` for private repositories and `https://travis-ci.org` for public repositories. The `.travis.yml` file specifies the build configuration for a project hosted on `https://travis-ci.org`; it enables Travis CI to learn about the project and how to build it. Create a new file in the `app/templates` directory named `travis.yml` if it doesn't exist, and add the following code:

```
language: node_js
node_js:
  - '0.10'
before_install:
  - 'bower install'
  - 'grunt build'
```

 For more information on Travis CI, visit `http://goo.gl/wMVg0c`.

The .gitattributes file for Git

The `.gitattributes` file specifies separate merging strategies for individual files and/or directories, and how Git runs a `diff` command on non-text files, or filters contents before a checkin/checkout. Create a new file in the `app/templates` directory named `gitattributes` if it doesn't exist, and add the following:

```
* text=auto
```

 For more information on Git attributes, visit `http://goo.gl/i4NwSQ`.

The .gitignore file for Git

The `.gitignore` file intentionally specifies untracked files and directories that Git should ignore and not add to the repository. Create a new file in the `app/templates` directory named `gitignore` if it doesn't exist, and add the following code:

```
app/bower_components/
node_modules/
.tmp/
.grunt
```

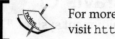 For more information on the Git ignore file,
visit http://goo.gl/OfSHGW.

Creating the .bowerrc file for Bower

The .bowerrc file specifies the installation directory of Bower components; it enables developers to manage Bower components in a custom directory location. Create a new file in the app/templates directory named bowerrc if it doesn't exist and add the following code:

```
{
    "directory": "app/bower_components"
}
```

The preceding code simply specifies in which directory Bower should install components into.

Creating the bower.json file for Bower

The bower.json file specifies the applications' dependencies, it enables developers to install, update, and remove application packages using the Bower package manager. Create a new file in the app/templates directory named _bower.json, if it doesn't exist, and add the following code:

```
{
    "name": "<%= _.slugify(siteTitle) %>",
    "version": "0.0.1",
    "main": [
        "app/scripts/main.js",
        "app/styles/main.css"
    ],
    "ignore": [
        "./node_modules",
        ".tmp",
        "app/bower_components",
        "app/images"
    ],
    "dependencies": {
        "jquery": "latest",
        "bootstrap": "latest",
        "handlebars": "latest"
    }
}
```

The preceding code does the following:

- It sets the `name` property to `siteTitle` that will be populated by the value from the prompts
- The `main` property defines the locations of the main files that should be only installed when using `bower install`
- The `ignore` property defines the locations that should be ignored when installing with `bower install`
- The `dependencies` property holds any Bower components that the project depends on

 For more information on configuring Bower, visit `http://goo.gl/R98hD4`.

Creating the application templates

The application-specific files will allow the user to run the app as well as have the files wired up and ready for logic. Let's take a look at the application level templates that will be created when the generator is invoked.

The index.html file

The `index.html` file is going to be the main application entry point; it will include default markup that will render the file in the browser upon initial page load.

The following is the content of the `app/templates/_index.html` file:

```
<!DOCTYPE html>
<html lang="en">
  <head>
    <meta charset="utf-8">
    <meta http-equiv="X-UA-Compatible" content="IE=edge,chrome=1">
    <meta name="viewport" content="width=device-width,
      initial-scale=1">
    <title><%= _.capitalize(siteTitle) %></title>
    <!-- bower:css -->
    <!-- endbower -->
    <link rel="stylesheet" href="styles/main.css"/>
  </head>
  <body>

    <article class="container slim">
      <header class="header">
```

```
        <nav>
          <ul class="nav nav-pills pull-right">
            <li class="active">
              <a href="#"> Home </a>
            </li>
          </ul>
        </nav>
        <h3 class="text-muted"><%= _.capitalize(siteTitle) %></h3>
        <hr/>
      </header>

      <section class="jumbotron center">
        <h1><%= _.capitalize(featureTitle) %></h1>
        <img src="<%= featureImage %>" alt=
          "<%= featureTitle %> image"/>
        <p class="lead">
          <%= _.capitalize(featureBody) %>
        </p>
      </section>
      <section class="page"></section>
    </article>

    <!-- bower:js -->
    <!-- endbower -->
    <script type="text/javascript" src="scripts/main.js"></script>
  </body>
</html>
```

The preceding code does the following:

- It declares the basic HTML5 site markup that contains templating and building tags, which get dynamically updated
- The `title` element inside the head uses the `_.capitalize` method from Underscore, which capitalizes the first letter of the `siteTitle`
- The `<!-- bower:css -->` comment is placed in the head where the installed Bower components' stylesheet files should get injected
- The markup used as the initial layout is referenced by the other projects created in earlier chapters using the templating syntax
- The `<!-- bower:js -->` comment is placed at the location where the installed Bower components' JavaScript files should go
- Then, at the very bottom, the main script for the application is declared, which will execute after the document is loaded

The main.css file

The `main.css` file is going to store the applications' styles. Here is the content of the `app/templates/_main.css` file:

```
/* Styles for <%= _.slugify(siteTitle) %> */
body{
  background: fefefe;
}
.slim{
  max-width:760px;
}
.center{
  text-align:center;
}
```

The preceding code does the following:

- A CSS comment is placed at the top that will be replaced by `siteTitle`
- Then some generic classes are declared that will adjust the background, width, and centering of text

The main.js file

The `main.js` file is going to store the applications' logic. It will create a global namespace with properties to store the created models, controllers, and views. Here is the content of the `app/templates/_main.js` file:

```
/* Script for <%= _.slugify(siteTitle) %> */
$(document).ready(function(){
  var App = {
    config: null,
    Models: {},
    Controllers: {},
    Views: {},
    init: function(){
      console.log('<%= _.capitalize(siteTitle) %> is ready to
        rock and roll!');
      return this;
    }
  };

  window.App = App.init();
});
```

The preceding code does the following:

- The `document.ready` function is used to execute the wrapped contents once the document is fully loaded
- The `App` variable is declared with some properties for storing `config`, `models`, `controllers`, and `views`
- The `init` method will simply log a message to the console and return the `App` object
- The `window.App` property is set to the `App.init()` method, which returns itself

Testing a custom generator

The generator-generator creates two example test files that will need to get modified to handle the prompts and files created when the `jps-site` generator is invoked. Yeoman does not set up any Grunt tasks for running the tests, so we are going to create a Gruntfile and populate it with tasks that will handle running unit tests and linting source files.

 The following steps assume that the current directory is `generator-jps-site`.

Setup

The first step will be setting up our testing environment, so that it will be easy to add more tests down the road. Perform the following steps:

1. First, add the following development dependencies to the `package.json` file in the generator's project directory:

```
"devDependencies": {
        "grunt": "^0.4.4",
        "grunt-contrib-coffee": "^0.10.1",
        "grunt-contrib-nodeunit": "^0.3.3",
        "grunt-contrib-jshint": "^0.9.2",
        "grunt-contrib-watch": "^0.6.1",
        "grunt-mocha-test": "^0.10.0",
        "grunt-contrib-clean": "^0.5.0",
        "load-grunt-tasks": "^0.4.0",
        "time-grunt": "^0.3.1",
        "chai": "^1.9.1",
        "mocha": "^1.18.2"
},
```

In the preceding code, we declared some development dependencies that will be installed by npm that allow us to create Grunt tasks for compiling and testing.

2. Next, create a file named `Gruntfile.js` in the custom generator's root directory. Open the `Gruntfile.js` file and add the following code:

```
'use strict';
  module.exports = function(grunt) {
    require('load-grunt-tasks')(grunt);
    require('time-grunt')(grunt);
    grunt.initConfig({
      clean: {
        test: ['test/temp']
      },
      watch: {
        compile: {
          files: ['app/*.js', 'test/*.js'],
          tasks: ['mochaTest']
        }
      },
      mochaTest: {
        test: {
          options: {
            reporter: 'spec'
          },
          src: ['test/**/test-*.js']
        }
      }
    });
    grunt.registerTask('default', ['clean', 'mochaTest']);
    grunt.registerTask('test', ['default']);
  };
```

The preceding code does the following:

- The `module.exports` property is set to a function that takes `grunt` as the argument, which allows access to the instance

- The `grunt.initConfig` method is invoked by passing an object of task-specific configuration settings

- The `clean` property declares a test target, which will remove any file and folder inside the `test/temp` directory

- The `mochaTest` property declares a test target, with options for reporting the `specs` run and `src` set to the location of the compiled files

- Finally, the `grunt.registerTask` method is invoked passing the name of the task (`default`) and subtasks to execute

Testing the generator output

The Yeoman API includes helpers for testing whether files exist, matching contents, and more. We are going to write a test that will execute the generator and ensure that the files created match the files expected. We will also match the content of those files against regular expressions to ensure that the values from the prompts are properly inserted in the correct locations.

The following specs are written in JavaScript. Create a new file `test-creation.js` in the `test` folder if it doesn't exist and add the following code:

```
'use strict';
var path = require( 'path' );
var helpers = require( 'yeoman-generator' ).test;
require( 'chai' ).should();

//Mocked questions and answers
var mockAnswers = {
  siteTitle: 'My Test Site',
  siteDesc: 'A modern site build to test.',
  featureTitle: 'Mocha Tests',
  featureBody: 'A modern site created by a Yeoman generator.',
  featureImage: 'http://goo.gl/SYjnUf'
};

//Mock expected files
var mockFiles = [
  '.bowerrc',
  'bower.json',
  '.gitattributes',
  '.gitignore',
  '.editorconfig',
  '.jshintrc',
  '.travis.yml',
  'Gruntfile.js',
  'package.json',
  'app/styles/main.css',
  'app/scripts/main.js',
```

```
    'app/index.html'
];

//Mock expected file contents
var mockFilePairs = [
  ['app/index.html',    RegExp( "<title>" + mockAnswers.
    siteTitle + "</title>" )],
];

describe( 'generator', function () {

  //Before each test clean the test/temp folder and create
    a new generator.
  beforeEach( function (done) {

    helpers.testDirectory( path.join( __dirname,
      'temp' ), (function (err) {
      if (err) {
        done( err );
      }

      //App generator
      this.app = helpers.createGenerator( 'learning-yeoman-ch6:app',
        ['../../app'], 'test-gen' );

      done();
    }).bind( this ) );
  } );

  //First test if the files that were created match what
    we expect.
  it( 'creates expected files', function (done) {

    //Add some mock prompts for the user to answer
    helpers.mockPrompt( this.app, mockAnswers );

    //Skip installing of the bower and npm dependencies
    this.app.options['skip-install'] = true;

    //Run the app and test for files and file contents
    this.app.run( {}, function () {
      helpers.assertFile( mockFiles );
      helpers.assertFileContent( mockFilePairs );
      done();
    } );
  } );
} );
```

The preceding code does the following:

- At the top of the file, some inline JSHint options are declared
- The `path`, `yeoman-generator`, and `chai` helpers are imported
- The `describe` block contains the content for testing
- The `mockAnswers` variable is set to an object of question name/value pairs that will get passed to the generator
- The `mockFiles` variable is set to an array of files expected to be created after the generator is invoked
- The `mockFilePairs` variable is set to an array of file/regex subarrays
- The `beforeEach` method will clean the `test/temp` folder and create a new generator instance
- The `it` method tests that the created files match the expected files
- The `mockPrompt` method is invoked on the helper passing in the generator instance and `mockAnswers`
- The `skip-install` option is set to true on the instance of the generator
- The generator instance is then run; in the callback function, the `assertFile` method is invoked passing the array of expected files
- The `assertFileContents` method is invoked on the helper, passing the array of `mockFilePairs` that will ensure contents are correct

Test generator loading

The load tests will check whether the generator can be initialized and loaded into the Node.js environment without breaking. Open the `test/test-load.js` file and add the following content:

```
'use strict';
var assert = require('assert');
require('chai').should();
  describe('jps-site generator', function() {
    it('can be imported without blowing up', function() {
        var app = require('../app');
        assert(app !== undefined);
      });
});
```

The preceding code does the following:

- At the top, it imports the `assert` and `chai` modules
- The `it` block will try and load the `app/index.js` module and assert that it is defined

To run the tests against the generator, you can use the following command:

`$ grunt`

After running this command, the result should look similar to the following screenshot:

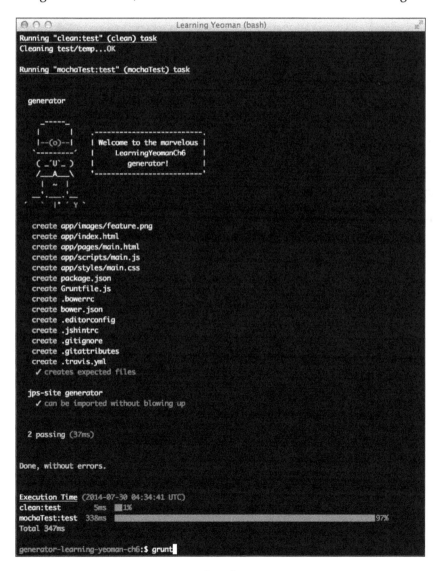

With the proper configuration, we can write generator unit tests and use Grunt to watch when source files change. The tests are run to ensure whether everything is working as expected.

The new custom subgenerator

Let's create a subgenerator for the custom generator we just created; this subgenerator is going to simply create a new page in the project and add a link to the page defined in the projects `app/index.html` file.

To create a new subgenerator, open a terminal and make the generator we created before the current working directory and execute the following command:

```
$ yo generator:subgenerator page
```

The preceding command will invoke the `generator:subgenerator` command, which then scaffolds a subgenerator module definition file and a template in the root of the generator project.

Understanding the subgenerator's directory structure

The directory structure created is relatively simple; it consists of a folder named after the subgenerator, an `index.js` file that contains the module definition, and a template in the `page/templates` directory:

```
page
├── index.js
└── templates
    └── somefile.js

1 directory, 2 files
```

The directory structure is broken down into the following:

- `page`: This folder is created and named after the subgenerator
  - `index.js`: This file contains the subgenerator module logic
  - `templates`: This folder contains the subgenerator template files
    - `somefile.js`: This is the default template that was scaffolded

The `somefile.js` file will be replaced with our actual template.

Creating subgenerator templates

Now that we have the initial subgenerator files, we need to create a custom template that will be copied into the target project when this subgenerator is invoked.

In the `page/templates` directory, create a new file named `_page.html` and add the following content:

```
<h1><%= name %></h1>
```

The content of the `page/_page.html` file is very simple; it only includes a Underscore.js templating expression to output the value of the passed name argument when the subgenerator was invoked.

Adding logic to the subgenerator

The logic for the subgenerator is very straightforward; the only responsibility the subgenerator has is to create a new file based on the name argument passed when invoking the subgenerator, and append a new link to the `app/index.html` file.

Open the `page/index.js` file and add the following content:

```
'use strict';
var util = require('util'), yeoman = require('yeoman-generator');

var PageSubGenerator = yeoman.generators.NamedBase.extend({

  //init - Initialize sub-generator
  init: function () {
    if (this.name) {
      return console.log('You called the page sub-generator
        with the argument' + this.name + '.');
    } else {
      throw new Error('You must provide a page name!');
```

```
    }
  },

  //files - Write the template to the projects app directory file
  files: function () {
    return this.copy('_page.html', 'app/pages/' + this.name +
      '.html');
  },

  //Handle appending a link to the index.html pages .nav element
  appendLink: function () {
    var htmlLink = '<li><a href="#/' + this.name + '">' +
      this.name + '</a></li>';
    return this.appendToFile('app/index.html', 'ul.nav',
      htmlLink);
  }
});
module.exports = PageSubGenerator;
```

At the top of the preceding code, the `util` and `yeoman` modules are included using the `require` method. The code comments to understand the logic this subgenerator provides.

Using your custom generator

When developing generators, it's always a good practice to try the generator out by yourself. As you don't have tons of issues logged in Github or another system, let's use it and create a simple website.

Link your generator

Now we need to link the custom generator to the system so that we can use the generator from the command line; from inside the root folder of the generator project, execute the following command:

npm link

The preceding command will add a symbolic link to your systems path, allowing you to run the `yo learning-yeoman-ch6` generator command from anywhere.

 For more information on npm link, visit `http://goo.gl/fwKa4Z`.

Scaffolding a new webapp

We are going to scaffold a website using the custom generator we created; open the terminal and perform the following steps:

1. Create the directory where your site will live and then execute the generator:

   ```
   $ yo learning-yeoman-ch6
   ```

   After running this command, the result will look like the following screenshot:

   After answering the questions, the files, shown in the preceding screenshot, are created and starts the installation of dependencies.

2. Now, you can start the server by running the following command:

   ```
   $ grunt serve
   ```

3. Your default web browser should open up displaying a page similar to the following screenshot:

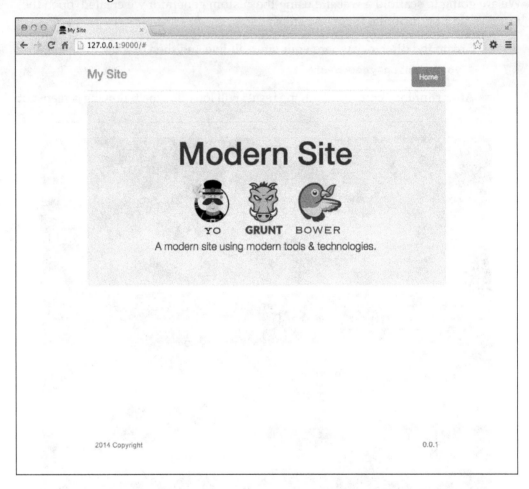

4. With a terminal window open, invoke the subgenerator and add the **About** page:

```
$ yo learning-yeoman-ch6:page About
```

 Watch LiveReload automatically refresh the browser and display your newly created link.

Self-test questions

The following are questions the reader should be able to answer by the end of this chapter:

1. Which command do you use to invoke a subgenerator?
2. What is the default templating library Yeoman uses to process templates?
3. What are the two types of code generators?
4. What two tests are created when invoking the Yeoman generator-generator?
5. What library is used to test Yeoman generators?
6. What prompting library does Yeoman use for its command prompts?
7. What are the four methods that are generated on the custom generator object?
8. Which class must you extend when creating a subgenerator?

Summary

This chapter covered creating custom Yeoman generators that take multiple answers from command line prompts and scaffold a modern web application. We used the API to download and install libraries from Bower into the application.

We covered writing tests that verify the directory structure and contents of files created dynamically based on user input, and publish the generator to npm for community usage. We also covered using the generator to create a simple test website and created custom Grunt tasks.

In the next chapter, we are going to look at creating custom libraries using Yeoman. We will create three libraries using the CommonJS generator, Node.js generator, and jQuery plugin generator.

7
Custom Libraries

In this chapter, we are going to cover how to create independent modules or plugins that can be used in a variety of ways such as a Node.js module, which will contain methods for creating a RESTful API server.

For the server side, we require a CommonJS module that will be used to handle the data store access, and then a jQuery plugin that will handle the client-side logic of performing CRUD operations via RESTful HTTP Ajax requests. We will write tests for these modules and use Bower and npm to publish them to the cloud for the npm community to consume.

In this chapter, we will cover the following topics:

- Using some of the official Yeoman generators to create different modules and plugins for different systems
- Creating a standard server-side JavaScript module in the form of CommonJS
- Creating a Node.js module that uses the same format as CommonJS
- Creating a jQuery plugin for usage in the browser
- The different types of modules and module loaders available on either the server or the client

The new CommonJS project

Using the Yeoman CommonJS generator, we will create a reusable module that can be consumed by other projects. This module will contain methods to perform CRUD (create, read, update, delete) operations. Let's get started!

Installing the generator-commonjs

To install the CommonJS generator, open a terminal and execute the following command:

```
$ npm install -g generator-commonjs
```

The preceding command will install the CommonJS generator globally on the system. You can use the yo commonjs command, which can be invoked anywhere.

Scaffolding a CommonJS project

To scaffold a new CommonJS project, open a terminal and do the following steps:

1. First, create the directory where the project is going to live, replace the jps attribute with your initials, and execute the following command:

   ```
   $ mkdir jps-ds && cd jps-ds
   ```

   The preceding command will create a new folder and make it the current directory.

2. Then, invoke the Yeoman generator inside the projects directory using the following command:

   ```
   $ yo commonjs
   ```

   The following actions are performed by the preceding command:

   - It prompts you with a series of questions about the module
   - It answers the questions as if you were the author
   - After answering the questions, the scaffold process will take place

The output from the preceding command should look similar to the following screenshot:

That's it! All the necessary files were just created in the current directory and include everything to get started writing module logic and unit tests. Now we are going to add the logic that will handle accessing the database.

To use this module during development in another project on the same machine, simply execute $ npm link as an administrator user to set the module in your PATH. Now, you will be able to use Node's require method to include this module from within any project during development.

The CommonJS logic

The logic for this module is going to be fairly straightforward; we will wrap the module in a function that takes one argument, that is, the options passed to the module. This module will have methods for connecting to the database, creating a new model instance, finding all records, finding one record, creating a record, updating a record, and removing a record.

This module is going to leverage Mongoose, which is a Node module for accessing MongoDB. The other module that we will use is Q, which provides a cross-platform solution for composing asynchronous promises in JavaScript. Perform the following steps:

1. Add the Mongoose module to the project, open a terminal, and execute the following command:

   ```
   $ npm install mongoose --save
   ```

   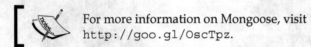 For more information on Mongoose, visit `http://goo.gl/OscTpz`.

2. Then, add the Q module to the project, open a terminal, and execute the following command:

   ```
   $ npm install q --save
   ```

 For more information on Q, visit `http://goo.gl/ZWFjnb`.

The preceding commands will download and install the packages into your `node_modules` folder inside the projects directory; the `--save` flag will add the entries to your project's `package.json` dependencies.

Module properties

The generator will create a skeleton file located in `learning-yeoman-ch7-commonjs/src` with the filename set to the name of the module specified during the generator prompts.

The module is wrapped in an immediately invoked function that passes in the global `exports` object. Some of the default properties need to be adjusted; so, open the `src/ds.js` file and add the following code:

```javascript
(function(exports) {
  'use strict';
  exports.DS = function(options){
      var mongoose = require("mongoose"),
          Q = require("q"),
          instance = null,
          models = {},
          ds = {};
  };
}(typeof exports === 'object' && exports || this));
```

The following actions are performed by the preceding code:

- An immediate invoking function wraps the entire module to ensure variables do not pollute any globals
- The DS property is set to a function on the exports object that takes one argument, that is, the options object to initialize this module with it
- The mongoose and q libraries are required and set to local variables
- The instance variable will handle keeping a reference of the current connection
- The models object will hold a reference to all the models when initialized
- The ds variable will hold all the methods that this module will expose to the public API

Connecting to MongoDB

The connect method will create model instances for each of the models passed in the options object and open a connection to the MongoDB database specified. Open the src/ds.js file and add the following code:

```
ds.connect = function (host) {
    if (options.models) {
      for (var m in options.models) {
        if (m) {
          var model = mongoose.model( m, new mongoose.Schema(
            options.models[m] ) );

                    models[m] = model;
        }
      }
    }
    instance = mongoose.connect( "mongodb://" + host );
    return this;
};
```

The following actions are performed by the preceding code:

- The connect method takes one argument, which is the mongo host location
- Inside the method body, we check if there is a models property on the passed arguments' options object

- If there are models, then a new model is created using the `mongoose.model` method by passing in the name of the model and `mongoose.Schema` that is created from the `models` object

- The newly created `mongoose` model instance is stored in the local `models` hash by name

Finding all models

The `findAll` method will handle fetching all records from the MongoDB database; this method returns a promise that will be resolved once the records are retrieved. Add the following code to the `src/ds.js` file:

```
ds.findAll = function (name) {
    var deferred = Q.defer();
    if (!models[name]) {
        throw new Error('Must add table to options.');
    }
    models[name].find( function (err, m) {
        if (!err) {
            deferred.resolve(m);
        } else {
            deferred.reject(err);
        }
    } );
    return deferred.promise;
};
```

The following actions are performed by the preceding code:

- The `findAll` method takes one argument, that is, the name of the collection

- If no model is found in the `models` hash object, then an error is thrown

- If there is a `model`, then the `find` method is invoked on that `model` instance and the promise is resolved by passing the items found

- If there is an error, then the promise is rejected passing in the `err` object

Finding a model

The `findOne` method will find a record by `id` and resolve the promise when found or reject if not found; add the following code to the `src/ds.js` file:

```
ds.findOne = function(name, id) {
    var deferred = Q.defer();
    if (!models[name]) {
        throw new Error('Must add table to options.');
```

```
    }
    models[name].findById( id, function (err, m) {
        if (!err) {
         deferred.resolve( m );
        } else {
         deferred.reject( err );
        }
    } );
    return deferred.promise;
};
```

The following actions are performed by the preceding code:

- The `findOne` method takes two arguments, which is the name of the collection and the ID of the document

- If no model is found in the `models` hash object, then an error is thrown

- If there is a model, then the `findById` method is invoked on the model instance that will then resolve the promise by passing in the object found from the method

- If there is an error while invoking the `findById` method, then the promise is rejected passing in the `err` object

Creating a model

The `create` method will handle creating a new document in the collection; to create a new document, all that is required is the name of the collection to insert into and the `data` object to insert.

Open the `src/ds.js` file and add the following content:

```
ds.create = function(name, data) {
    var deferred = Q.defer();
    if (!models[name]) {
        throw new Error('Must add table to options.');
    }

    var model = new models[name](data);
    model.save(function(err, m) {
        if (!err) {
            deferred.resolve(m);
        } else {
            deferred.reject(err);
        }
    } );
    return deferred.promise;
};
```

The following actions are performed by the preceding code:

- The `create` method takes two arguments, the name of the collection and the `data` object to insert
- If no model is found in the `models` hash object, then an error is thrown
- If there is a model, then the `save` method is invoked on the `model` instance by passing in the `data` object to create, which resolves the promise after that
- If an error occurs while invoking the `save` method, then the promise is rejected passing in the `err` object

Updating a model

The `update` method will handle updating a document in the collection found by the ID of the document. To update a document, just pass in the name of the collection, the ID of the document, and a `data` object of `key:value` pairs to update.

Open the `src/ds.js` file and add the following content:

```
ds.update = function (table, id, data) {
    var deferred = new Deferred();
    if (!models[name]) {
        throw new Error('Must add table to options.');
    }
    models[table].findByIdAndUpdate( id, data, function (err, m) {
        if (!err) {
            deferred.resolve( m );
        } else {
            deferred.reject( err );
        }
    } );
    return deferred.promise;
};
```

The following actions are performed by the preceding code:

- The `update` method takes three arguments, the name of the collection, the ID of the document, and the properties to update
- If no model is found in the `models` object hash, then an error is thrown
- If there is a model, then the `findByIdAndUpdate` method is invoked on the model instance passing in the ID and the data to update; when finished, the promise will be resolved with the results from the method
- If an error occurs, then the promise will be rejected passing in the `err` object

Destroying a model

The `delete` method will handle removing a document from a collection; all that is required is the name of the collection and the ID of the document from which to remove. Open the `src/ds.js` file and add the following code:

```
ds.destroy = function (table, id) {
    var deferred = Q.defer();
    if (!models[name]) {
        throw new Error('Must add table to options.');
    }
    models[table].findByIdAndRemove( id, function (err, m) {
        if (!err) {
            deferred.resolve( m );
        } else {
            deferred.reject( err );
        }
    } );
    return deferred.promise;
};
if (options.host) {
    return ds.connect( options.host );
} else {
    return ds;
}
```

The following actions are performed by the preceding code:

- The `destroy` method takes two arguments, the name of the collection and the ID of the document
- If no model is found in the `models` object hash, then an error is thrown
- If there is a model, then the `findByIdAndRemove` method is invoked by passing the ID of the document to destroy, and the promise is resolved by passing the response from the method
- If an error occurs, then the promise will be rejected by passing in the `err` object

Testing a CommonJS project

The CommonJS Yeoman generator includes nodeunit as the default test framework. The specs for the module are located in the test directory; using this test framework is fairly simple.

[For more information on nodeunit, visit `http://goo.gl/vHzSyG`.]

Open the test spec that is located at `test/ds_test.js` and add the following code:

```
'use strict';
var DS = require( '../src/ds.js' ).DS;

var _ds = new DS( {
    host: 'test:test@ds037498.mongolab.com:37498/learning-yeoman',
    models: {
        'pages': { title: String, body: String}
    }
} );

var _page, _pages, _id;

exports['DS'] = {
    setUp: function (done) {
        done();
    },
};
```

The following actions are performed by the preceding code:

- At the top of the file, the module that we are testing is imported using the `require` method
- Then, the `_ds` variable is set to a new instance of the DS module, passing in an `options` object that contains the mongo host
- The `models` property is set to an object that defines the collections' structure
- The `_page` variable will hold a reference of the page that will be used for testing
- The `_pages` variable will hold a reference of all the pages that are returned from the module
- The `_id` variable will hold a reference of the model created for deleting it as well
- The global `exports` object has the DS property, which is the name of the module that we were testing
- The `setUp` function will run before each key in the object and is used to set up the model before running tests

Test for no model

The module should throw an error if there is no model instance created before calling a method on the table. Open the `test/ds_test.js` file and add the following code:

```
'noTable': function (test) {
    test.expect( 1 );
    test.throws( function () {
        _ds.findAll( 'null-table' );
    }, Error, 'should throw Error if no table' );
    test.done();
},
```

The following actions are performed by the preceding code:

- The `noTable` property is declared, which is set to a function that takes a `test` argument, which is an instance of nodeunit
- The `expect` method is called, declaring that there should be one test expectation
- The `throws` method is called with a function that will invoke the `findAll` method by passing a table that does not exist
- The module should throw an error if no table is found prior being invoked
- The `done` method is called to inform nodeunit that the test is complete

Test finding all models

To ensure that the module can return the proper data when the `findAll` method is invoked, open the `test/ds_test.js` file and add the following code snippet to the `DS` object:

```
'findAll': function (test) {
    test.expect( 1 );
    _ds.findAll( 'pages' ).then( function (data) {
      _pages = data;
      test.ok( (data instanceof Array) );
      test.done();
    } );
},
```

The following actions are performed by the preceding code:

- The `findAll` property is declared, which is set to a function that takes a `test` argument, which is an instance of nodeunit
- The `expect` method is called, declaring that there should be one test expectation

- Then, the findAll method is invoked with the pages argument that will set the _pages variable to the returned data

- Inside the then method, the ok method is called to ensure the data object is an instance of the Array class

- The done method is called to inform nodeunit that the test is finished

Test finding one model

The findOne method should return an object, so let's create the spec. Open the test/ds_test.js file and add the following code snippet to the DS object:

```
'findOne': function (test) {
    test.expect( 1 );
    _id = _pages[0]._id;
    _ds.findOne( 'pages', _id ).then( function (data) {
    _page = data;
    test.ok( (data instanceof Object),
        'should return object.' );
      test.done();
    });
},
```

The following actions are performed by the preceding code:

- The findOne property is declared and is set to a function that takes a test argument, which is an instance of nodeunit

- The expect method is called, declaring that there should be one test expectation

- The _id variable is set to the first object's ID in the results from the findAll method called before

- Then, the findOne method is invoked with the _id argument that sets the _page variable to the object returned

- Inside the then method, the ok method is called to ensure the _page object is an instance of the Object class

- The done method is called to inform nodeunit that the test is finished

Test creating a model

The module should be able to create a new model, so we will write a spec for that. Open the test/ds_test.js file and add the following code to the DS object:

```
'create': function (test) {
    test.expect( 1 );
```

```
        _page = {
            title: 'Page ' + Date.now(),
            body: 'This is the page content.',
            published: true,
            created: new Date()
        };
        _ds.create( 'pages', _page ).then( function (data) {
            test.ok(data._id, 'should return object with id.' );
            test.done();
        } );
    },
```

The following actions are performed by the preceding code:

- The create property is declared, which is set to a function that takes a test argument, which is an instance of nodeunit
- The expect method is called, declaring that there should be one test expectation
- The create method is invoked on the module, passing in the _page object that was constructed
- Inside the then function, the ok method is used to test that the data returned from the module has an _id object, which will be the newly created model
- The done method is called to inform nodeunit that the test is complete

Test updating a model

The module should be able to update an existing model; open the test/ds_test.js file and add the following code to the DS object:

```
'update': function (test) {
    test.expect( 1 );
    _page = {
        title: 'Updated Page'
    };
    _ds.update( 'pages', _id, _page ).then( function (data) {
        test.equal( data.title, 'Updated Page',
            'should have updated title.' );
        test.done();
    } );
},
```

The following actions are performed by the preceding code:

- The `update` property is declared, which is set to a function that takes a `test` argument, which is an instance of nodeunit
- The `expect` method is called, declaring that there should be one test expectation
- The `update` method is called on the `pages` model, passing in the `_id` variable and the update `_page` object
- Inside the `then` function, the `equal` method is used to ensure the returned value from the module is the same value that was updated
- The `done` method is called to inform nodeunit that the test is complete

Test destroying a model

The module should be able to delete a model; open the `test/ds_test.js` file and add the following to the DS object:

```
'destroy': function (test) {
    test.expect( 1 );
    _ds.destroy( 'pages', _page._id ).then( function (data) {
        test.equal( data, true, 'should return object.' );
        test.done();
    } );
}
```

The following actions are performed by the preceding code:

- The `destroy` property is declared, which is set to a function that takes a `test` argument, which is an instance of nodeunit
- The `expect` method is called, declaring that there should be one test expectation
- The `destroy` method is called on the `pages` model, passing the ID of the updated model used before
- Inside the `then` function, the `equal` method is used to ensure the data returned is true, signifying a successful deletion
- The `done` method is called to inform nodeunit that the test is complete

To run the tests, execute the following command:

```
$ grunt nodeunit -v
```

The preceding command will output something similar to the following screenshot:

The default `grunt` command will build and test the module; different tasks can be added to the `Gruntfile.js` file, easily allowing the use of more tasks.

Deploying to npm

Deploying the newly created module is fairly straightforward using npm, which is a package manager for managing Node dependencies. You need to authenticate first by running the `$ npm adduser` command. To publish this module to npm, use the following command:

```
$ npm publish
```

Your module will then show up in results from the `npm search` command, if the criteria matches that defined in the modules `package.json` file.

Conclusion

In this section, we have learned about the CommonJS module format and how to create modules that can be used on the server side. We covered the basics of setting up testing.

The new Node.js module project

We can easily scaffold node modules using the Yeoman Node.js generator; all projects include nodeunit unit tests. The generator is based on the `grunt-init-node` module, authored by the magnificent GruntJS team.

Installing the generator-node

To install the Node.js generator, execute the following command:

```
$ npm install -g generator-node
```

The preceding command will install the Node.js generator globally on the system. Now, the `yo node` command can be invoked anywhere.

Scaffolding a Node.js module project

First create a new directory and make that the current working directory. To quickly scaffold a new Node.js module project, execute the following command:

```
$ yo node
```

The preceding command will prompt you with a series of questions about the plugin. After answering the questions, the scaffold process will take place.

The output from the preceding command should look similar to following screenshot:

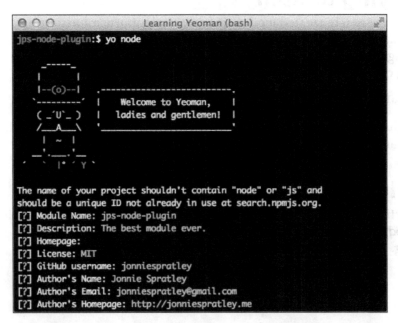

You can answer the questions as if you are the plugin author. For demonstration purposes, you can use any information you like; just be sure to make the proper naming changes when following the code examples.

The Node.js module logic

The logic for this module is very straightforward; it will consist of a simple Node. js server that will handle GET/PUT/POST/DELETE HTTP calls from the client. The module will return an instance of an Express server that can be used in any application.

Before we can start writing the module logic, we need to install the module's dependencies. Open a terminal and execute the following command:

```
$ npm install supertest express body-parser --save
```

The preceding command with download and install the `supertest`, `express`, and `body-parser` modules from npm and will add them to the project's `package.json` dependencies array.

Open the `lib/jps-node-plugin.js` file and add the following content:

```
'use strict';
exports.RestServer = function() {
    var express = require('express'),
      bodyParser = require('body-parser'), server = express();
    server.use(bodyParser.json());
};
```

The following actions are performed by the preceding code:

- On the global `exports` object, a `RestServer` module function is declared that will house the logic for the module
- Next, `express` is loaded via the `require` method along with the `body-parser` module
- Then, a new `express` instance is created, which is set to the private `server` variable

Now that the module definition is in place, we can start adding methods that will handle incoming HTTP requests. Inside the module definition, add the following code:

```
server.get('/api', function (req, res) {
  res.json({message: 'RESTful Node API Server'});
});

server.get('/api/:table', function (req, res) {
  res.json({message: 'Query items in ' + req.params.table});
});

server.post('/api/:table', function (req, res) {
  res.json({message: 'Create item in ' +
    req.params.table});
});

return server;
```

The following actions are performed by the preceding code:

- At the top, the entire module is wrapped inside a function that is declared on the exports object
- The name of the module is the name of the property that is declared on the exports object, which is a function that will return the server object
- The server object contains handlers that will accept HTTP requests in the form of GET and POST
- For example, each call will just return a message of what it is supposed to do in JSON; you can actually extend this further with logic that does what you desire

 For more information on Express, visit http://goo.gl/0qEBVX.

Testing a Node.js module

The Yeoman Node.js generator sets up testing with the nodeunit framework and makes it easy to write unit tests for custom node modules; since we are going to be testing an HTTP server, we are going to use the supertest module that will handle sending example requests to the server and then make sure the response from the server is what we are expecting.

Open the `test/jps-node-plugin_test.js` file and add the following content:

```
var RestServer = require('../lib/jps-n.js').RestServer;
var request = require('supertest'),
   mockServer,
   expected = {
     message: 'RESTful Node API Server'
   };
//Start mock servermockServer = new RestServer();mockServer.
listen(9090);
//Listen to mock server
exports.RestServer = {
   setUp: function(done) {
     done();
   },
   'GET /api/posts': function(test) {
     expected.message = 'Query items in posts';
      request(mockServer).get('/api/posts').expect('Content-Type',
        /json/).expect(200).end(function(err, res) {
       if (err) {
         throw err;
       }
       test.deepEqual(res.body, expected, 'should get all items');
       test.done();
     });
    },
   'POST /api/posts': function(test) {
     expected.message = 'Create item in posts';
     request(mockServer).post('/api/posts').expect('Content-Type',
       /json/).expect(200).end(function(err, res) {
       if (err) {
         throw err;
       }
       test.deepEqual(res.body, expected, 'should create item');
       test.done();
     });
   }
};
```

The following actions are performed by the preceding code:

- At the top of the file, the `request` variable references the `supertest` module that is imported using the `require` method

- Then, we start a mock server by invoking the `listen` method on the module that we created earlier

- The tests are declared on the global `exports` object; the keys for the specs and the values are functions, which get invoked for every spec
- There will be two test cases, which are as follows:
  - The first spec will test if the default route will return the message that is expected
  - The GET /api/posts spec will send a GET request to the server and expect that the response is what we expect
  - The POST /api/posts spec will send a POST request to the server along with an object we wish to create; the response should match the expected message set above the request call

To run the unit tests, open the terminal and execute the following command:

```
$ grunt -v
```

The default `grunt` task will lint and test the module displaying the results from the tests in the console, as seen in the following screenshot:

```
● ○ ○                    Learning Yeoman (bash)
Testing jps-node-plugin_test.js
RestServer - GET /api/posts...{}
OK
RestServer - POST /api/posts...{}
OK

>> 2 assertions passed (238ms)

Done, without errors.


Execution Time (2014-07-24 21:47:14 UTC)
loading tasks       408ms    ████████████████57%
jshint:gruntfile     33ms    ██5%
jshint:lib           16ms    █2%
jshint:test          15ms    █2%
nodeunit:files      241ms    ████████34%
Total 715ms

jps-node-plugin:$ ▌
```

 For more information on SuperTest, visit `http://goo.gl/GjiJAc`.

Deploying

Since this is a Node.js module, the only logical place to deploy this module would be the Node's package manager (npm); to publish this package to npm, use the following command:

```
$ npm publish
```

The preceding command will register your `package.json` file into the npm repository, allowing your module to be installed and updated using npm.

[For more information on deploying, visit `http://goo.gl/g4LuCP`.]

Conclusion

That was easy; now you should have an understanding on what a CommonJS module is and how to create one using the Yeoman CommonJS generator. We covered setting up a new CommonJS project, writing a unit test to verify the code works, and publishing the module to the npm repository. Now, you should be able to create CommonJS modules with ease and publish them to the npm repository.

The new jQuery project

Let's create a new jQuery project that will demonstrate using the Yeoman jQuery generator to quickly create a reusable plugin, which is fully tested and deployed to Bower for consumption by others in the community. This plugin will simply call CRUD methods on the client side by creating utility methods that aid in sending GET/PUT/POST/DELETE requests to the server and handling the response accordingly. Let's get started.

This generator is based on grunt-init-jquery, authored by the magnificent GruntJS team.

Installing the generator-jquery

To install the jQuery generator, open the terminal and execute the following command:

```
$ npm install -g generator-jquery
```

The preceding command will install the jQuery generator globally on the system. Now, the `yo jquery` command can be invoked anywhere.

Scaffolding a jQuery project

First create a new directory and make that the current working directory. To scaffold a new jQuery project, open a terminal and execute the following command:

```
$ yo jquery
```

The following actions are performed by the preceding command:

- It will prompt you with a series of questions about the plugin
- Answer the questions as if you were the author of this plugin
- After answering the questions, the scaffold process will take place, logging the output to the console as the files are created and the dependencies are downloaded

If you answered the questions, then you should see something similar to the following screenshot:

```
                                    Learning Yeoman (bash)
jps-plugin:$ yo jquery


     ------
    |      |
    |--(o)--|      .------------------------------.
    `--------'     |    Welcome to Yeoman,        |
    ( _`U`_ )      |    ladies and gentlemen!     |
    /___A___\      '------------------------------'
     |  ~  |
   __`.___.'__
 `  \  |° ' Y `

_Project Name_ should not contain "jquery" or "js" and should be a unique ID not already in
use at plugins.jquery.com.

_Project title_ should be a human-readable title, and doesn't need to contain the word "jQue
ry", although it may.

For example, a plugin titled "Awesome Plugin" might have the name "awesome-plugin".

For more information, please see the following documentation:

Naming Your Plugin       http://plugins.jquery.com/docs/names/
Publishing Your Plugin   http://plugins.jquery.com/docs/publish/
Package Manifest         http://plugins.jquery.com/docs/package-manifest/
[?] Project Name: jps plugin
[?] Title: Awesome jQuery plugin
[?] Description: The best jQuery plugin ever.
[?] Version: 0.0.1
[?] Repository: https://github.com/jonniespratley/learning-yeoman-ch7/blob/master/jps-plugin
[?] Bugs:
[?] License: MIT
[?] Github Username: jonniespratley
[?] Author Name: Jonnie Spratley
[?] Author Email: jonniespratley@gmail.com
[?] jQuery Version: 2.x
```

Adding the plugin logic

We are going to create the client-side adapter for the plugin that will handle sending objects to the server side for processing; the file that will handle the routing logic will be the CommonJS module we created earlier in the chapter. The server-side routes will be the Node.js modules that we created in the new Node.js project.

Let's go ahead and open the `src/jps-plugin.js` file and add the logic that will handle sending requests to the server:

```
(function ($) {
    var crud = {
        endpoint: '/api',
        create: function (table, data) {
            return this._send( 'POST', table, data );
        },
        read: function (table, data) {
            return this._send( 'GET', table, data );
        },
        update: function (table, data) {
            return this._send( 'PUT', table, data );
        },
        destroy: function (table, data) {
            return this._send( 'DELETE', table, data );
        },
        query: function (table, params) {
            return this._send( 'GET', table, params );
        },
        _send: function (type, table, data) {
            var url;
            url = this.endpoint + "/" + table;
          if (data != null ? data.id : void 0 &&
            type !== 'GET') {
              url += '/' + (data != null ? data.id : void 0);
            }
            return $.ajax( {
                url: url,
                type: type,
                dataType: "json",
                data: data
            } );
        }
    };

    $.extend( $.fn, {
        crud: crud
    } );
})( jQuery );
```

The following actions are performed by the preceding code:

- The script looks similar to the CommonJS module created earlier, except that we are setting our plugin methods on the query object instead of the exports object.

- This is a self-invoking function that passes a reference of query to the constructor that will be used to set the plugin methods and options.

- The first method is set on the $ object, which is a function that takes an object of plugin options that will extend with the default options defined in the plugin.

- The create method will be invoked using $.crud.create(), which will take two arguments: the name of the collection and the object to create. The method will return a promise that is resolved upon response from the server.

- The read method will be invoked using $.crud.ready(), which will take two arguments: the first is the name of the collection and the second is the object to find; if null, it will find all objects in the collection. This method returns a promise that will be resolved once a response from the server is sent.

- The update method will be invoked using $.crud.update, which will take two arguments: the first is the name of the collection and the second is the object to update. This method will also return a promise that will be resolved once received from the server.

- The destroy method will be invoked using $.crud.destory, which will take two arguments: the first is the name of the collection and the second is the object to remove. This method will return a promise that is resolved once sent from the server.

Testing a jQuery plugin

The Yeoman jQuery generator sets up testing configuration for the plugin that includes the QUnit testing framework. Since this plugin interacts with the server by sending HTTP requests, having a way to mock the responses from the server is generally recommended, as we do not know if there is a server available to send our requests to and keeping everything local while running unit tests will speed up the time.

 For more information on QUnit, visit http://api.qunitjs.com/.

Before we start writing the spec, install the `jquery-mockajax` library. Open the terminal and execute the following command:

```
$ bower install jquery-mockajax --save-dev
```

The following actions are performed by the preceding command:

- It will download and install the `jquery-mockajax` library into the `bower_components` directory
- Then, it will add the library to the `devDependencies` object in the `bower.json` file

Now, add the `jquery-mockajax` library to the test spec runner located in the `test/test-plugin.html` file and add the following script tag that includes the jQuery Mockjax library:

```
<script src="../bower_components/jquery-
   mockajax/jquery.mockjax.js"></script>
```

 For more information on jQuery Mockjax, visit `http://goo.gl/wkGACb`.

Creating the unit test

Now that we have installed the Ajax mocking library, the next step would be to add the mock methods to the test spec. Open the test spec located at `test/jps-plugin_test.js` and add the following code:

```
/* global module, asyncTest, jQuery, expect, equal, start */
(function ($) {

    var expected = {
        create: 'Create item in posts',
        query: 'Query items in posts'
    };

        module('$.fn.crud', {
        setup: function() {
        $.mockjax({
          url: '/api/*',
          type: 'GET',
          responseText: {
            message: expected.query
          }
```

```
      });
    $.mockjax({
      url: '/api/*',
      type: 'POST',
      responseText: {
        message: expected.create
      }
    });
  }
});
```

The following actions are performed by the preceding code:

- The entire spec is an immediate function that will pass jQuery as the parameter
- The `expected` object contains the results that we are expecting; the keys in the object represent the method and the value represents the expected value
- The `module` method creates a new spec; the first argument (`$.fn.crud`) is the name of the test and the second parameter is an object containing the `setup` function that is used for bootstrapping the spec before it is run

Now, we are ready to write a few tests to verify that the plugin is returning the data that we are expecting; open the `test/jps-plugin_test.js` file and add the following code:

```
//Should make a POST request to the server sending the data.
asyncTest ( 'create', function () {
    expect ( 1 );
    $.fn.crud.create ( 'posts', {name: 'test',
      body: 'This is a test.'} ).done ( function (data) {
        equal ( data.message, expected.create,
          'should return data' );
        start ();
    } );
} );

//Should make a GET request to the server.
asyncTest ( 'query', function () {
    expect ( 1 );
    $.fn.crud.query ( 'posts' ).done ( function (data) {
        equal ( data.message, expected.query,
          'should return data' );
        start ();
    } );
} );

}( jQuery ));
```

The following actions are performed by the preceding code:

- The `asyncTest('create')` method will handle verifying whether the `$.crud.create()` method makes the proper request and returns the correct response. The `start` method is called to inform QUnit that the async operation is complete and it is good to proceed.

- The `asyncTest('update')` method also handles verifying whether the `$.crud.update()` method makes the property request, and inside the `done` method, the results are compared to the expected update object to match, again calling the `done` method when complete.

- The same process goes for the `destroy` method, as well, making the call and comparing the results with the expected value.

To run these unit tests, open a terminal and execute the following command:

```
$ grunt test
```

The output from the command should look similar to the following screenshot:

You can also run these tests in the browser by opening the `test/jps-plugin.htm` file in any browser of your choice.

Deploying to Bower

The jQuery plugin will be deployed to Bower; this allows the library to easily be updated whenever a new version is available. To deploy the plugin to bower.io's repository, perform the following steps:

1. The first step is to create the `bower.json` file by running the following command:

   ```
   $ bower init
   ```

   The following actions are performed by the preceding command:

   ◦ It will initialize a new `bower.json` file and ask you a series of questions about the library

   ◦ The prompts are already set up with the expected default values; confirm each entry by pressing *Enter*

2. Next, you need to register the plugin by executing the following command:

   ```
   $ bower register [name] [url]
   ```

   The preceding command will register the plugin's name and URL with Bower. The URL is generally the location of the repository but can reference a .zip file or other resource.

3. To validate that your plugin is now registered with Bower's repository, open a terminal and execute the following command:

   ```
   $ bower search [plugin-name]
   ```

   The preceding command will send a `search` query to bower.io and return any results that match the [name] argument, as demonstrated in the following screenshot:

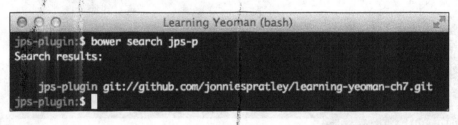

Conclusion

Creating a jQuery plugin is fun and pretty easy, but using the Yeoman jQuery plugin generator makes it even easier. In this section, we covered installing and scaffolding a plugin project using the jQuery generator. Now that you have created a jQuery plugin with unit tests and published to Bower, the sky is limit.

Self-test questions

The following are questions that you should be able to answer after reading this chapter:

1. What is a package manager?
2. What is a command-line interface?
3. How do you register a package on Bower?

Summary

We have covered how to create different modules and plugins for different systems using some of the official Yeoman generators. We began by creating a standard server-side JavaScript module in the form of CommonJS; we also created a Node.js module that uses the same format as CommonJS. We covered creating a jQuery plugin for usage in the browser.

We also got acquainted with the different types of modules and module loaders available on either the server or client. This should give you enough ammo to create some useful plugins that are available for the community.

In the next chapter, we are going to cover how to use Grunt, the JavaScript task runner.

8
Tasks with Grunt

This chapter will cover using Grunt, the JavaScript task runner; we will install and set up Grunt in new or existing projects. We will use Yeoman generators to automate the processes of automating a project.

There are a number of benefits of using Grunt in your everyday development workflow. We are going to cover what Grunt is and how to utilize the various tasks for managing projects as well as adding Grunt to existing projects. Let's get started!

In this chapter, we are going to cover the following topics:

- The basics of Grunt and how to add it to a new or existing project
- The Yeoman Grunt plugin generator to create a plugin that is published to npm

Overview on GruntJS

Grunt is a JavaScript task runner for managing tasks during development. Grunt runs in the Node.js environment and provides a quick solution over other build tools because of the huge ecosystem of plugins, which add additional functionality to the command line. Grunt is an alternative to Ant or Make.

Grunt tasks are JavaScript modules that utilize the Node and Grunt API to add automation in just about anything; tasks are installed using Node's package manager npm.

Grunt eases the management of a project by performing various tasks and can help manage a project's life cycle from development to production.

[For more information on GruntJS, visit http://goo.gl/XA9qnz.]

Installing the Grunt CLI

In order to use the grunt command, you will need to install Grunt's command-line interface (CLI) globally on your system. Open a terminal and execute the following command:

```
$ npm install -g grunt-cli
```

The preceding command will download and install grunt-cli on your system and wire up the grunt command in your system path. This does not install the Grunt task runner; the CLI is only responsible for running the version of Grunt that is specified in a project's package.json file relative to the Gruntfile.js file. This enables different projects to use different versions of Grunt without getting affected.

 The -g flag generally requires an administrator user.

Installing Grunt

The easiest way to add Grunt to your project is with the npm install command, which will download and install the plugin into your project's node_modules folder and add the entry to your project's package.json file. Open a terminal and execute the following command:

```
$ npm install grunt --save-dev
```

The preceding command will install Grunt and save the devDependencies property to the package.json files.

 This assumes that the project has a package.json file in the root.

Grunt usage

To use Grunt, the command format is as follows:

```
$ grunt [task [...]] [options]
```

The preceding command will execute the task(s) specified by passing in the specified options to invoke the tasks.

Grunt options

The grunt command comes with many options to choose from when invoking tasks; the options available are as follows:

Option	Description
-h, --help	This displays the help text
--no-color	This disables all colored output
--gruntfile	This specifies an alternative Gruntfile
-d, --debug	This enables debugging mode on tasks that support debug mode
-f, --force	This forces tasks to complete through warnings and errors
--tasks	This displays an additional directory to scan for tasks
--npm	This scans node_modules for Grunt plugin tasks
-v, --verbose	This displays the detailed output log
-V, --version	This displays the current Grunt version
--completion	This outputs autocompletion shell rules

Installing the generator-gruntfile

The Yeoman Gruntfile generator will streamline setting up Grunt in an existing or new project. To install, open a terminal and execute the following command:

```
$ npm install -g generator-gruntfile
```

To use this generator, execute the following command:

```
$ yo gruntfile
```

The output from this command will look similar to the following screenshot:

The questions the generator asks will help it decide on whether the DOM is involved; it will set up QUnit and if not, it will add nodeunit. If files in the project need to be minified, then the generator will set up tasks to do that.

After the execution of command is finished, you should have a new `Gruntfile.js` file and `package.json` file located in the current working directory.

Using Grunt

To set up Grunt, either with a new project or an existing project, there are only two very important files that are needed to add the Grunt JavaScript task runner.

The package.json file

The `package.json` file is the file that contains the project's dependencies and development dependencies that are generally Grunt tasks. Take a look at the following `package.json` file:

```
{
    "name": "learning-yeoman-ch8",
    "version": "0.0.0",
    "dependencies": {},
    "devDependencies": {
```

```
    "grunt": "~0.4.2",
    "grunt-contrib-watch": "~0.5.3",
    "grunt-contrib-concat": "~0.3.0",
    "grunt-contrib-uglify": "~0.2.7",
    "grunt-contrib-jshint": "~0.7.2",
    "grunt-contrib-qunit": "*"
  }
}
```

This file simply defines the project configuration settings and then specifies the project's dependencies; the Grunt tasks are located in the devDependencies property, which specifies what Grunt task plugins are required for this project.

The Gruntfile.js file

The Gruntfile.js file is the file that contains the configuration settings for tasks in your project. Take a look at the following example:

```
grunt.initConfig({
    concat: {
        options: {},
        foo: {},
        bar: {
            options: {}
        }
    }
});
```

The following actions are performed by the preceding code:

- The grunt.initConfig method is invoked by passing in task options
- The concat task is configured with global options overriding the task defaults
- The foo property is a target of the task that sets target-level options
- The bar property is a target of the task that will use the task-level options

Loading tasks

Grunt handles loading tasks that are specified in the Gruntfile.js file using the loadNpmTasks method, as follows:

```
grunt.loadNpmTasks('grunt-contrib-concat');
```

The preceding code is placed inside the `Gruntfile.js` file right below the `module.exports = function(grunt)` method and will load the Grunt task by the passed name. The tasks are loaded by performing a lookup inside the `node_modules` directory relative to the current working project's directory.

Creating the alias tasks

Grunt also supports the ability to create alias tasks that can be used to execute multiple tasks by creating an alias task, which invokes all subtasks that are defined in the alias. For example, consider the following code:

```
grunt.registerTask('customTask', ['qunit', 'concat', 'uglify']);
```

The following actions are performed by the preceding code:

- It uses the `registerTask` method to register a new task named `customTask` that will execute the tasks in the order specified in the second argument
- The usage of invoking this newly registered task goes in the form of the following command:

  $ grunt customTask

  The preceding command will invoke the custom registered task, thus running all tasks defined in the task list array.

 For more information, visit `http://goo.gl/PvNbZf`.

Multiple target tasks

Grunt has the ability to run multiple tasks with multiple configurations; each task that is declared in the `Gruntfile.js` file can have any number of **target** tasks, which are just aliases for running the task with different configuration options, as follows.

A task such as `concat:dist` or `uglify:dist` will do the following:

- It will only process the files specified in the tasks' `dist` target options
- Then each target specified inside that task will be executed, which allows you to have more control over which tasks and targets will be run with different files

 For more information on multiple task targets, visit `http://goo.gl/urjOkA`.

Registering the basic tasks

Grunt will execute the basic tasks without looking at the configuration or environment and will just run the task function by passing in any specified colon-separated arguments to the task function as arguments. For example, consider the following code snippet:

```
grunt.registerTask(taskName, [description, ] taskFunction)
```

The preceding code registers a new task named `taskName` with an optional description and function to invoke when that task is run.

> For more information on creating basic tasks, visit http://goo.gl/yUvkNT.

Options – files

Most tasks perform file operations, so Grunt has included a powerful abstraction layer for declaring which files the task should operate on. There are many ways to define the file mappings that are used when running the tasks.

For example, take a look at the following task target options:

```
grunt.initConfig({
    myTask: {
        staticFiles: {
            files: [{
                src: 'src/myfile.js',
                dest: 'build/myfile.min.js'
            }]
        }
    }
});
```

The following actions are performed by the preceding code:

- The `grunt.initConfig` method is invoked by passing an object of installed tasks configuration settings
- The `myTask` property specifies the options for the task, with a target of `staticFiles`
- The `files` property for the target task is set to an array of file objects that have properties specifying the source (`src`) and destination (`dest`) for the input/output of the files

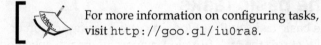

For more information on configuring tasks,
visit http://goo.gl/iu0ra8.

Options – file patterns

The `files` property of Grunt supports the `node-glob` file pattern, which allows you to use the following options:

- `*`: This option matches any number of characters but not the / directory slash
- `?`: This option matches a single character but not the / directory slash
- `**`: This option matches any number of characters, including / if it's the only character
- `{}`: This option matches a comma-separating list of expressions
- `!`: This option matches the beginning of a pattern with a negative match

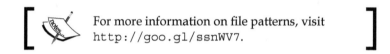

For more information on file patterns, visit
http://goo.gl/ssnWV7.

Options – dynamic patterns

To build the file options of your tasks dynamically, you can use template strings in the file property values, which can be used in both compact and the files array formats. When you set the `expand` property to `true`, the following options become available:

- `cwd`: This sets the current working directory where files are matched from
- `src`: This specifies the patterns to match relative to the `cwd` property
- `dest`: This specifies the destination file path
- `ext`: This replaces the file extension specified in the `dest` property
- `extDot`: This is used to specify the period location of the file extension, either `first` or `last`
- `flatten`: This will remove all file paths from the generated `dest` path
- `rename`: This is a function that will be invoked for each file, which matches the `src` property
- `dest`: This is a function that will be invoked with each `src` and `dest` of every file matched in the `src` property; this function must return the new destination

For example, take a look at the following Grunt task:

```
grunt.initConfig({
  myTask: {
    dynamicFiles: {
      files: [
        {
          expand: true,
          cwd: 'lib/',
          src: ['**/*.js'],
          dest: 'build/',
          ext: '.min.js',
          extDot: 'first'
        }
      ]
    }
  }
});
```

The following actions are performed by the preceding code:

- The `grunt.initConfig` method is invoked with an object of task settings
- The `myTask` property specifies the options for the task
- The `dynamicFiles` property is the target and files of the task, which use the `expand` property to enable extra options for dynamic file lookups
- The `cwd` property sets the `lib` folder as the director to perform the file lookups
- The `src` property sets the source of the files to any file nested inside the directory with the `.js` file extension
- The `dest` property sets the location of the processed files to be placed by the task
- The `ext` property sets the new extension for each file that is processed by the task
- The `extDot` property specifies the extension that begins after the `first` dot in the filename

 For more information on dynamic file objects, visit `http://goo.gl/7b0E6o`

Options – templates

By default, Grunt supports Lo-Dash template expressions that are specified using the
`<%= %>` syntax. Grunt will automatically expand each task recursively until no more
tasks or targets remain. You can dynamically create filenames and contents using
templates and also provide support for methods in templates, as follows:

```
<%= grunt.template.today('yyyy-mm-dd') %>.
```

The preceding code will invoke a date and time helper method on the
`grunt.templates` object by passing in a date pattern that will be executed,
and return the current date in that given format.

 For more information on templates, visit `http://goo.gl/2GPAjc`.

Options – importing data

Grunt also supports importing external data that can be in either a JSON or YAML
format. The following methods can be used to import existing external data for your
grunt tasks:

- `grunt.file.readJSON`: This method will load the file specified as JSON
- `grunt.file.readYAML`: This method will load the file specified as YAML

 For more information on importing formats, visit
`http://goo.gl/DWn1W4`.

The new project

The easiest way to add Grunt to a new project is to use a Yeoman app generator. The
most common generator to use with a generic project would be the generator-webapp,
which will create all the necessary files and configure some general tasks to build and
test your code.

To use a Yeoman generator, execute the following command:

```
$ yo [generator_name]
```

The preceding command will invoke the generator in the current directory by
creating all files needed for development along with fully configured Grunt tasks
ready for use.

My custom Grunt plugin

Now that we have an overview on using Grunt and the power that it can bring to a new or existing project, let's use the Yeoman Grunt plugin generator to create a custom Grunt plugin that will allow the use of custom created tasks in any project.

Installing the generator-gruntplugin

To install the Yeoman Grunt plugin generator, execute the following command:

```
$ npm install -g generator-gruntplugin
```

The preceding command will install the Grunt plugin generator globally on your system, allowing the use of the `yo gruntplugin` command from within any directory.

Usage

To use the Grunt plugin generator, execute the following command:

```
$ yo gruntplugin
```

The directory structure

The directory structure that is created contains very few files and modules by default, but your plugin can include any Grunt task installed into the project. Take a look at the directory structure created by Yeoman:

```
├── Gruntfile.js
├── README.md
├── node_modules
│   ├── grunt
│   ├── grunt-contrib-clean
│   ├── grunt-contrib-jshint
│   ├── grunt-contrib-nodeunit
│   ├── jshint-stylish
│   └── load-grunt-tasks
├── package.json
├── tasks
│   └── learning_yeoman_ch8.js
└── test
    ├── learning_yeoman_ch8_test.js
    ├── expected
    └── fixtures
```

The generator scaffolds the directory structure as follows:

- `Gruntfile.js`: This contains Grunt tasks to use on the plugin
- `README.md`: This contains project-specific information including installation and usage of the plugin
- `node_modules`: This contains the module dependencies used by the plugin
- `package.json`: This contains project information including repository location, main script paths, start and stop commands, and npm dependencies
- `tasks`: This contains the source files for the plugin tasks
- `test`: This contains the test specs for the plugin that will be run against the module:
  - `expected`: This directory contains the expected files that the plugin produces
  - `fixtures`: This directory contains sample files that the plugin will load for testing

The Grunt plugin logic

The plugin logic is located in the `tasks/learning_yeoman_ch8.js` file that gets created by Yeoman during the initial scaffold; open the file and add the following code:

```
'use strict';
module.exports = function(grunt) {
  function LearningYeomanCh8() {
    //Plugin logic here
  };
  grunt.registerMultiTask(
    'learning_yeoman_ch8',
    'This is an example plugin.',
    LearningYeomanCh8
  );
};
```

The following actions are performed by the preceding code:

- The `module.exports` property is set to a function, which takes `grunt` as the only argument
- Inside the `exports` method, the plugin's main function is declared and will encapsulate the logic of the plugin
- The task is then registered by invoking the `registerMultiTask` method by passing in a description and the constructor function of the plugin

When registering a plugin as a multi-task, this enables the task to iterate over every target specified in the configuration settings. If no target is specified when invoking the custom task, then each target in the task is executed.

Plugin options

Tasks generally have a set of default options, which they use when performing some type of logic. To specify default options for your plugin, add the following code inside the module method:

```
var options = this.options( {
  template: 'Hello <%= name %>',
  data: {
    name: 'Learning Yeoman'
  }
} );
```

The following actions are performed by the preceding code:

* It declares an `options` variable that is set to the current task's target options
* If no options exist in that target, then the defaults are specified
* If a task's target has options, then the task will use those options instead

Using Grunt to read files

Tasks generally take input files and process them, so your plugin should have methods for checking whether the file path exists before trying to read the content. Open the `tasks/learning_yeoman_ch8.js` file and add the following code inside the main function:

```
var checkFiles = function (filepath) {
  if (!grunt.file.exists( filepath )) {
    grunt.log.warn( 'Source file "' + filepath + '" not found.' );
    return false;
  } else {
    return true;
  }
};
var readSource = function (file) {
  return file.src.filter( checkFiles ).map( function (filepath) {
    return grunt.file.read( filepath );
  } ).join( grunt.util.normalizelf( '' ) );
}
```

In the preceding code, the `files.forEach` method is invoked internally on the `this.files` property.

Since all tasks involve the file system, the files property is the files that are populated from the options in the task configuration; using file globbing patterns the files are added to the local instance of the task.

Using Grunt to write files

Since tasks usually manipulate files in some sort of way, writing the output of those files should be included.

Open the `tasks/learning_yeoman_ch8.js` file and add the following code inside the `LearningYeomanCh8` function:

```
var readWriteFile = function (file) {
  var src = readSource( file );
  src += grunt.template.process(
    options.template,{data: options.data}
  );

  grunt.file.write( file.dest, src );
  grunt.log.writeln( 'File "' + file.dest + '" created.' );
};
// Iterate over all specified file groups.
this.files.forEach(function(file) {
  readWriteFile(file);
});
```

The following actions are performed by the preceding code:

- The `src` variable is set to the results from the `readSource` method, which will return the content of the file passed
- Then the compiled fragment returned from invoking the `grunt.template.process` method will be added to the source files
- Then the `grunt.file.write` method is invoked by passing `file.dest`, which will be the `dest` set in the task options along with the new contents of the file
- The last method will log a message to the console when the task is complete
- Finally the last three lines bring this plugin together by invoking `readWriteFile` for each file that is matched from the tasks file settings

Testing a Grunt plugin

The Yeoman generator creates the testing configuration and an example spec that is located in the `test/learning_yeoman_ch8_test.js` file; open the file and examine the content, which should look like the following:

```
'use strict';
var grunt = require('grunt');
exports.learning_yeoman_ch8 = {
  setUp: function (done) {
    // setup here if necessary
    done();
  },

 //default options test - should write 'Hello Learning Yeoman'
   by default.
   default_options: function(test) {
     test.expect(1);
     var actual = grunt.file.read('tmp/default_options');
     var expected = grunt.file.read('test/expected/default_options');
     test.equal(actual, expected, 'should perform task with
       default options.');
     test.done();
   },

 //custom options test - should write 'Hello [name]' where [name] is
 the value.  custom_options: function(test) {
     test.expect(1);
     var actual = grunt.file.read('tmp/custom_options');
     var expected = grunt.file.read('test/expected/custom_options');
     test.equal(actual, expected, 'should perform task with custom
       options.');
     test.done();
   }
};
```

The preceding code:

- At the top, the `grunt` variable is assigned to the `grunt` module.

- The `exports` object defines the test suite; in this case,
  it's `learning_yeoman_ch8`.

- This object has three properties; the first is `setUp`, a function that is ran
  during the initialize phase and any initializing logic should go here.

- The second property is `default_options`; this tests the plugin and creates
  the correct file content that matches the plugins `default_options`.

- The third property is `custom_options`; this tests the plugin and creates the
  correct file content that matches the plugins `custom_options`.

Creating test fixtures

Since tasks in Grunt generally modify the filesystem or file(s) in some way or another, creating fixtures allows you to test whether your plugin is performing the correct logic.

Open the `test/fixtures/default_options` file and modify it to the following:

```
Hello Learning Yeoman
```

The preceding code is the value that is set up as the default value in the `tasks/learning_yeoman_ch8.js` file.

Open the `test/fixtures/custom_options` file and modify it to the following:

```
Hello Jonnie
```

The preceding code is the value that is set in the `Gruntfile.js` file, under the `learning_yeoman_ch8.custom_options` task. This is the value we are expecting the plugin to add to the created files.

Running the tests

Now that we have a test spec and fixtures, we are ready to test the plugins functionality. To run the nodeunit tests, open the terminal and execute the following:

```
$ grunt test -v
```

The preceding command will execute the test task specified in the `Gruntfile.js` file and display something similar to the following screenshot:

Deploying to npm

The custom plugin is ready to publish on npm for community usage. To publish your package, execute the following command:

```
$ npm publish
```

This command will register the package with npm and is now ready to install anywhere.

Usage

To use this task, all that is required is to install the module using npm and then add the configuration options to your project's `Gruntfile.js` file. For example, here are the steps:

1. Install the plugin and save it to your `package.json` file; execute the following command:

    ```
    $ npm install learning-yeoman-ch8 --save-dev
    ```

2. Add the task options to your Gruntfile, as follows:

    ```
    learning_yeoman_ch8 : {
        default_options : {
          files : {
            'tmp/default_options' : ['test/fixtures/default',
              'test/fixtures/custom']
          }
        },
        custom_options : {
          options : {
            data :{
              name: 'Jonnie'
            }
          },
          files : {
            'tmp/custom_options' : ['test/fixtures/default',
              'test/fixtures/custom']
          }
        }
    }
    ```

3. Finally, execute the task by executing the following command:

    ```
    $ grunt learning_yeoman_ch8
    ```

Self-test questions

The following are questions that the reader should be able to answer at the end of this chapter:

1. Which command is used to list all the available Grunt tasks?
2. Which are the three most common Grunt tasks?
3. What type of environment does Grunt run in?
4. How to execute a target Grunt task?
5. How do you register a new Grunt task?
6. How to install a new Grunt task?
7. What are the alternatives to Grunt?

Summary

In this chapter, we covered the basics of Grunt and how to add it to a new or existing project. We also utilized the Yeoman Grunt plugin generator to create a plugin that is published to npm. Now that we have covered creating and configuring tasks for modern web development, the sky is the limit.

In the next chapter, we will learn a few important Yeoman tips and tricks.

9
Yeoman Tips and Tricks

In this chapter, we will cover some useful tips and tricks that one might need when using Yeoman and some of the generators. We will improve the existing projects that we created earlier by adding code coverage to our projects, as well as creating a RESTful Node server that will communicate to a MongoDB database using the module we created in the previous chapter.

While this is not an extensive list of tips and tricks, it does consist of some very detailed steps that will help with adding functionality to any project—not just the ones covered in this chapter.

Some common issues that developers run into while using the different Yeoman generators are as follows:

- Accessing server-side resources because of cross-domain scripting issues
- Configuring, running, and creating e2e (end-to-end) UI tests
- Configuring and generating code coverage reports from unit tests

In the sections to come, we will tackle these problems and come up with usable solutions that will make developing web applications, using any of the generators, a lot smoother.

Let's get started!

Webapp generator solutions

When creating a generic web application using the Yeoman generator-webapp, it would be nice to have a remote server somewhere serving all the API endpoints for the app to consume. However, since JavaScript cannot simply make HTTP calls to remote domains without some type of cross-site scripting setup, having a proxy server that can integrate with the Connect server while developing will make life a lot easier. It allows you to start writing code without having to wait for the server team to set up custom proxy scripts in order to access the endpoints.

Creating a RESTful Node.js server

Problem: Your project requires RESTful API routes that map resources to a MongoDB database to perform basic CRUD (create, read, update, and delete) operations and return the results in a JSON format.

Solution: Create a Node.js server by installing Express and the `jps-ds` module from *Chapter 7, Custom Libraries*; since that module contains methods for performing CRUD operations on a MongoDB data source, we can easily leverage the module to speed up development. As for the server routes, we can easily use Express, which is a Node.js module, as well. Then, it's a matter of connecting the dots and starting the server. Let's get started!

Installing module dependencies

First, install the dependences using `npm`. Open the terminal and execute the following command:

```
$ npm install jps-ds express body-parser --save
```

The preceding command will download and install both `jps-ds` and `express`, and then save the modules to the project's `package.json` file.

Creating the server

Now, create a `server.js` file that will contain the routes and logic. The server will handle taking request parameters and invoke the corresponding methods on the data source.

Configuring the server

Now, we need to import the modules that allow us to create an express server that will handle the routes for the application. Open the `server.js` file and add the following code:

```
var application_root = __dirname,
    express = require('express'),
    path = require('path'),
    bodyParser = require('body-parser'),
    app = express(),
    DS = require('jps-ds').DS,
```

```
    port = process.env.PORT || 5000;

//Setup static directory
app.use(express.static(application_root + '/dist'));

// parse application/json
app.use(bodyParser.json());
```

The following actions are performed by the preceding code:

- At the top of the file, private variables are declared and set to some required modules, such as `express`, `path`, `bodyParser`, and `jps-ds`

- The `app` variable creates a new instance of an `express` app

- The DS variable stores a reference to the DS module created in the earlier chapter

- The `bodyParser.json()` method tells express to parse the request body as content-type `application/json` and populate the `request.body` property with the value

- The `express.static` method tells express in what directory to serve static content

Configuring the data source

Now, we need to configure the data source settings so that it can connect to the MongoDB database and make queries. Open the `server.js` file and add the following code below the server configuration:

```
var _ds = new DS({
  host: 'localhost/learning-yeoman',
  models: {
    'posts': {
      title: String,
      slug: String,
      body: String,
      image: String,
      published: Boolean,
      tags: Array,
      created: Date,
      modified: Date
    }
  }
});
```

The following actions are performed by the preceding code:

- It defines a _ds variable that will hold a reference to the DS module instance; passing an object to the module will configure the module

- The host property is set to a local installation of MongoDB that should be running in the background

- The models property is an object where the key is the name of the table or collection and the value is the fields for that collection

- That's the configuration needed for accessing the MongoDB resource since this module provides a layer of abstraction

Defining server routes

Now, it's time to define the routes for the application and add the logic that will invoke the DS module to gather data to be returned by the express app when the route is matched and processed.

The default route

The default route will simply return a message to the user; open the server.js file and add the following code:

```
app.get('/api', function (request, response) {
  response.send({message: 'API is running'});
});
```

The following actions are performed by the preceding code:

- The /api route is registered, so that when the URL is hit, it will return an object that contains a message stating the API is running

- The response.send method will handle sending the object to the browser as JSON

GET – fetch the posts route

For the GET route that will handle fetching all posts from the MongoDB database, open the server.js file and add the following code:

```
app.get('/api/posts', function (request, response) {
  _ds.findAll('posts').then(function(data){
    return response.send(data);
  });
});
```

The following actions are performed by the preceding code:

- The `/api/posts` route is registered, so that when the URL is requested with a GET method, it will call the `findAll` method on the DS module passing in the name of the collection

- Since the method is a promise, the `then` method handles the response by sending the data to the browser

POST – create the post route

Now, for the POST route that will handle creating a post in the MongoDB database, open the `server.js` file and add the following code:

```
app.post('/api/posts', function (request, response) {
  _ds.create( 'posts', {
    title: request.body.title,
    body: request.body.body,
    published: request.body.published,
    created: new Date()
  } ).then( function (model) {
    return response.send(model);
  } );
});
```

The following actions are performed by the preceding code:

- The `/api/posts` route is registered, so that when the URL is requested with a `post` method, it will call the `create` method on the DS module passing in the object to send to the backend

- The object that is sent to the `create` method is extracted from `request.body`; since `express` parsed the body and made it an object, we can easily access properties by using dot syntax

- After the model is saved to the database, the browser is given with the results from the `create` method

- The `response.send` method will handle sending the object to the browser as JSON

GET – a single post route

Now, for the GET route that will find one post in the MongoDB database by the post ID, open the `server.js` file and add the following code:

```
//Get a single by id
app.get('/api/posts/:id', function (request, response) {
```

```
    _ds.findOne('posts', request.params.id).then(function(data){
      return response.send(data);
    });
  });
```

The following actions are performed by the preceding code:

- The `/api/posts/:id` route is registered, so that when a GET request is sent to the URL with an ID parameter, it will call the `findOne` method on the DS module

- The `findOne` method will find the record where the ID matches and returns the object

- The `response.send` method will handle sending the object to the browser as JSON

PUT – update the post route

Now, for the PUT route that will handle updating a post in the MongoDB database by the post ID, open the `server.js` file and add the following code:

```
app.put('/api/posts/:id', function (request, response) {
  _ds.update( 'posts', request.params.id, {
    title: request.body.title,
    body: request.body.body,
    image: request.body.image,
    tags: request.body.tags,
    published: request.body.published
  } ).then( function (model) {
    return response.send(model);
    console.log( 'model updated', model );
  } );
});
```

The following actions are performed by the preceding code:

- The `/api/posts/:id` route is registered, so that when the URL is requested with a PUT method and has an ID parameter in the URL, it will call the `update` method on the DS module

- The `update` method takes three arguments: the table name, the ID of the object to update, and the object to send to the database to update

- The method returns a promise that will be resolved when complete

- The `response.send` method will send the object to the browser as JSON

DELETE – remove the post route

Now, for the DELETE route that will remove a post from the MongoDB database by the post ID, open the `server.js` file and add the following code:

```
//Delete
app.delete('/api/posts/:id', function (request, response) {
  _ds.destroy( 'posts', request.params.id).then( function (data) {
    return response.send(data);
  } );
});
```

Starting the server

Now, it's time to start the server so that we can test these routes and make sure that they are correctly handling requests. Open the `server.js` file and add the following code snippet at the bottom of the file:

```
var port = 9090;
app.listen(port, function () {
  console.log('listening on port %d in %s mode', port,
    app.settings.envenv);
});
```

The preceding code simply creates a port variable set to `9090` and invokes the `listen` method on the `express` app, which will start the server.

Running the server

Now, we are all ready to run this node server so that requests to the endpoint will react accordingly. Open the terminal and execute the following command:

```
$ node server
```

The preceding command will run the server.js file and display the log output in the console.

Testing the server

Now, we are ready to test if the server handles the requests properly. Let's send the server some requests and check if we get what we are expecting. You could write a unit test for this, but to demonstrate quickly, let's just use `curl` to send the requests.

Open the terminal and execute the following commands to test the server:

1. Test the default endpoint:

```
$ curl -i -H "Accept: application/json" http://localhost:9090/api
```

2. Test to get all posts:

```
$ curl -i -H "Accept: application/json" http://localhost:9090/api/
posts
```

3. Test to create a post:

```
$ curl -i -H "Accept: application/json" http://localhost:9090/api/
posts
```

4. Test to update a post:

```
$ curl -i -H "Accept: application/json" -X PUT -d "title=cURL
Updated&body=Updated post content&image=http://placehold.it/200"
http://localhost:9090/api/posts/5341d503527b01000072a2cc
```

5. Test to remove a post:

```
$ curl -i -H "Accept: application/json" -X DELETE http://
localhost:9090/api/posts/5341b957527b01000072a2cb
```

Setting up the proxy server

Now, we are ready to install and configure the json-proxy module that will handle allowing you to route all API calls to a local or remote server based on the matching prefix in the requested URL. It will make more sense when we implement this proxy; open the terminal and execute the following command:

```
$ npm install json-proxy --save-dev
```

The preceding command will download and install the json-proxy node module that will enable you to use a proxy server during development.

Configuring the proxy server

Now, we need to configure the proxy server so that all HTTP calls that match a certain criteria will be forwarded to a URL of our choice. Open the Gruntfile.js file and add the following to the connect:livereload task options; the middleware function that is declared is where you want to insert the following code:

```
//Around line #55
connect:{
  livereload: {
    options: {
      middleware: function(connect) {
```

```
        return [

            //Import and configure the json-proxy module.
            require( 'json-proxy' ).initialize( proxyConfig ),
            ...

        ];
     }
   }
 }
}
```

The preceding code will handle importing and initializing the `json-proxy` module with the specified configuration; so when the `connect:livereload` server task is ran, this proxy server will be up and running listing on the same port. Add the following to the top of the `Gruntfile.js` file that declares the settings for the proxy module:

```
var serverEndpoint = 'http://jonniespratley.me:8181/api/v2/learning-
yeoman';
var proxyConfig = {
 proxy: {
  forward: {
    '/api': serverEndpoint
  }
 }
};
```

The preceding code simply declares a `serverEndpoint` variable that holds the location of the API server we will route HTTP calls to. The `proxyConfig` object has a proxy `property`.`forward` property that specifies the context in which to forward requests to when matched, the value is `serverEndpoint`, which is the API endpoint we wish to forward all requests made with `/api` in the URL.

To use this proxy server, simply start the Grunt connect live reload server by running the following command:

```
$ grunt serve
```

Conclusion

It took only nine steps and we were able to get a RESTful Node server up and running, talking to a MongoDB database that can perform CRUD operations, which are accessed through a proxy server.

Angular generator solutions

The most common issue with Angular apps is setting up e2e testing. Well, let's cover setting up Protractor with an Angular app, so we can run e2e tests to verify that the application is functioning as it should.

Protractor e2e testing

Problem: I have an AngularJS app that was created using Yeoman and I want to add Protractor e2e testing to my project. I want to run a Grunt task that will start Protractor and execute my project's e2e test specs.

Solution: In order to properly test your AngularJS application using Protractor, you will need to perform the following steps in this order:

1. Install `protractor` using `npm`.
2. Install `grunt-protractor-runner` using `npm`.
3. Configure the Grunt task.
4. Create a Protractor configuration file.
5. Create an e2e test spec.
6. Start Selenium WebDriver.
7. Start the application.
8. Run the Grunt task.

Installing Protractor

To install Protractor, you must use npm and install it globally, as follows:

```
$ npm install protractor -g
```

Now, update the Selenium WebDriver using the web driver manager. Open the terminal and execute the following command:

```
$ webdriver-manager update
```

The preceding command will invoke `webdriver-manager` that comes bundled with Protractor to update the required files needed to run the Selenium WebDriver.

 It will download `chromedriver` and Selenium Server's `.jar` files to the installation directory of Protractor, which, on a Linux or Mac system, lives in `/usr/local/lib/node_modules/protractor`. You might need to adjust the permissions of the `protractor` directory.

Installing the grunt-protractor-runner

Now, you will need to install the Grunt task to run the Protractor tests; open the terminal and execute the following command:

```
$ npm install grunt-protractor-runner --save-dev
```

The preceding command will download and install the grunt-protractor-runner node module to the node_modules directory and add the entry to your project's package.json file.

Configuring the Protractor task

Now, let's configure the Grunt task. Open the Gruntfile.js file and add the following at the bottom of the task settings object:

```
protractor : {
  options : {
    keepAlive : true,
    noColor : false,
    args : {}
  },
  test : {
    options : {
      configFile : "e2e.conf.js"
    }
  }
}
```

The following actions are performed by the preceding code:

- It configures the grunt-protractor-runner task by setting up some options that will be passed to the protractor instance
- The test target defined inside the protractor task will be the configuration file that is loaded by Protractor when running this task

Creating the Protractor configuration

Now, you need to create the configuration file for Protractor. Open the terminal and execute the following command:

```
$ touch e2e.config.js
```

Open the `e2e.config.js` file and add the following content:

```
exports.config = {
  seleniumAddress : 'http://localhost:4444/wd/hub',
  capabilities : {
    'browserName' : 'chrome'
  },
  baseUrl : 'http://localhost:9090',
  specs : ['test/e2e/*.js', '.tmp/e2e/*-e2e.js'],
  jasmineNodeOpts : {
    isVerbose : true,
    showColors : true,
    includeStackTrace : true,
    defaultTimeoutInterval : 30000
  }
};
```

The following actions are performed by the preceding code:

- The `config` property is set on the global `exports` property
- The `seleniumAddress` property is set to the location of the Selenium Server instance that is running
- The `capabilities` property is an object that sets the capabilities of the browser
- The `baseUrl` property is set to the location of the web server that is hosting the application
- The `specs` property is an array that contains the location of the specs; you can use file globbing patterns for including specs
- The `jasmineNodeOpts` property is an object that contains settings that will be passed to the Jasmine node module when Protractor is running
- The `isVerbose` property is set to `true` so that all logging will display in the console; the `showColors` property will allow color logs to be enabled
- The `includeStackTrace` property is set to `true` so that the console will log stack trace errors
- The `defaultTimeoutInterval` is used for specifying the default number of milliseconds before the spec fails

Creating an e2e spec

Now, we need to create an e2e test spec that will handle loading the application and checking if the pages contain what we are expecting. Open the `test/e2e/app.coffee` file and add the following code:

```
var Config = {
  baseurl: "http://localhost:9000/#",
  sitetitle: "learning yeoman",
  sitedesc: " a starting point for a modern application.",
  sitecopy: "2014 Copyright",
  version: '0.0.1',
  email: "admin@email.com",
  debug: true,
  feature: {
    title: 'Chapter 3',
    image: /img/learning-yeoman/yo-ng.png',
    body: 'A starting point for a modern angular.js application.'
  }
};
```

The following actions are performed by the preceding code:

- At the top, a `Config` object is created that holds values, which should be in the application
- This is the same `Config` object that was used in all previous chapters; so I assume you are familiar with it by now

The MainPage object

Since it is a best practice to create page objects that contain properties and methods for the corresponding page, let's create a `MainPage` object that will hold properties and a method for loading the page.

Open the `test/e2e/app.coffee` file and add the following code:

```
MainPage = ->
  @sitetitle = element(protractor.By.binding("App.sitetitle"))
  @featureTitle =
    element(protractor.By.binding("App.feature.title"))
  @featureDesc =
    element(protractor.By.binding("App.feature.body"))
  @features = element(protractor.By.binding("App.features"))
  @get = ->
    return browser.get("http://localhost:9000/#")
  @name = 'MainPage'
```

The following actions are performed by the preceding code:

- The `MainPage` is a function that contains some properties and methods
- The `sitetitle` is set to the `element` selector by binding, which looks for `{{App.sitetitle}}` in the view
- The `featureTitle`, `featureDesc`, and `features` properties are also set to the `element` selector by binding
- The `get` method will handle loading the correct URL in the browser
- The `name` property is set to the name of the page object

The PostPage object

Now, let's create a `PostPage` object that will hold properties to reference the form inputs in the page and some methods for loading the different views populating the form.

Open the `test/e2e/app.js` file and add the following:

```
PostPage = ->
  @title = element(protractor.By.model('post.title'))
  @body = element(protractor.By.model('post.body'))
  @image = element(protractor.By.model('post.image'))
  @tags = element(protractor.By.model('post.tags'))
  @published = element(protractor.By.model('post.published'))
    @submitBtn =
      element(protractor.By.css('button[type="submit"]'))
  @get = ->
    return browser.get(Config.baseurl + '/posts')
  @getNew = ->
    return browser.get(Config.baseurl + '/posts/new')
  @getEdit = (id)->
    return browser.get(Config.baseurl + '/posts/edit/' + id)
  @edit = (id) ->
    @editBtn =
      element(protractor.By.css("[data-id=\"#{id}\"] .edit"))
    @editBtn.click()
  @form = (p)->
    @title.sendKeys(p.title)
    @body.sendKeys(p.body)
    @image.sendKeys(p.image)
    @tags.sendKeys(p.tags)
    @submitBtn.click()
    browser.sleep(1500)

  @name = 'PostEditPage'
```

The following actions are performed by the preceding code:

- It creates a new `PostPage` object that will contain properties and methods for the post page
- The `title` property is set to the `element` selector by model, which will look for `ng-model=post.title` in the view
- The `getNew` method will simply load the new post page into the browser
- The `getEdit` method will simply load the edit post page into the browser
- The `edit` method takes one argument, that is, the ID of the model to edit
- The `form` method takes one argument that is an object; when invoked, the method will call the `sendKeys` method on the elements that were selected by the model value
- Then, the `submitBtn.click()` method is invoked, which will submit the form followed by the `browser.sleep` method to inform Protractor to wait about 1.5 seconds before proceeding

The e2e spec

Now, the test spec will use the page objects along with the assertion methods to handle testing the values retrieved from the page objects.

Open the `test/e2e/app.coffee` file and add the following code:

```
describe 'Chapter3 e2e:', ->
  mainPage = new MainPage()

  describe "the main page", ->
    beforeEach ->
      mainPage.get()

    it "should have site title and description", ->
      expect(mainPage.sitetitle.getText())
              .toEqual(Config.sitetitle)
      expect(mainPage.featureTitle.getText())
              .toEqual(Config.feature.title)
      expect(mainPage.featureDesc.getText())
              .toEqual(Config.feature.body)

  describe 'the new post page', ->
    postPage = new PostPage()
    beforeEach ->
```

```
        postPage.getNew()

    it 'should create a post', ->
        expect(browser.getCurrentUrl())
                .toEqual(Config.baseurl + '/posts/new')
        postPage.form({
                title: Test -' + new Date().toString(),
                body: 'Test post body',
                tags: 'protractor,angular,test',
                image: 'http://placehold.it/200'})
        expect(browser.getCurrentUrl()).toEqual(Config.baseurl +
            '/posts')
```

The following actions are performed by the preceding code:

- The `describe` block wraps the entire content in a test suite
- A `mainPage` variable is defined and set to a new instance of the `MainPage` object
- Then, the `describe` block encloses the content in a main page test suite
- The `beforeEach` method will invoke the `get` method on the `mainPage` object, which will load the web page
- The `it` spec will handle testing if the page has a site title, feature title, and description by calling the `getText()` method
- The third `describe` block encloses the post page spec, and the `beforeEach` method will load the `posts/new` web page
- The `it` spec will check if the post form can create a new post
- The expectation is that the current URL is /`posts/new`, and then calling the `form` method on the post page object and passing an object with properties to send to the form
- After the post is saved, the expectation is that the `/posts` route is loaded to display all posts in the database

Starting the Selenium WebDriver

Now, in order to run Protractor, you need to have the Selenium Server running in the background; this is done by starting it with the web driver manager that Protractor installed. To start the Selenium Server, open the terminal and execute the following command:

```
$ webdriver-manager start
```

The preceding command will start the Selenium Server and output the logging information such as the host it is running on, which is `http://127.0.0.1:4444/wd/hub`.

Starting the application

Now that the web driver is running, you can start your application; open another terminal and execute the following command:

```
$ grunt serve
```

 The preceding command will start the Connect server launching Chrome, displaying your application that was created earlier. The tutorial is present in *Chapter 3, My Angular Project*.

Running e2e tests

To run the e2e tests, you will need to modify your `Grunfile.js` file so that the CoffeeScript is compiled before the tests run; so open the `Gruntfile.js` file and add the following code snippet to the bottom of the file:

```
grunt.registerTask('test:e2e', ['test', 'protractor']);
```

The preceding code will register a new task that will first run the test task to clean and compile the source files, and then launch the e2e tests using Protractor.

Now, to run your e2e tests, you can just run the following command:

```
$ grunt test:e2e
```

This command will run all tests followed by launching Chrome and Protractor to test the application end-to-end.

Backbone generator solutions

This section covers some solutions that one might need when using the Backbone generator.

Code coverage with Karma

Problem: You want to run your project's unit tests with Karma and generate code coverage for your project.

Solution: Since you want to use Karma and leverage the karma-coverage plugin, you will need to create and configure a `test/test-main.js` file that will parse all the indexed files and create an array of spec files that are then added to the Require.js configuration as dependencies. After all the files have been indexed, you will need to start Karma so the specs can be run. To do so, perform the following steps:

Installing Karma and plugins

Since the Yeoman Backbone generator creates a Karma configuration file located in the root of the project directory by default, all that is needed is to install the karma-coverage plugin and enable it in your `karma.conf.js` file.

To install karma-coverage, open the terminal and execute the following command:

```
$ npm install karma-coverage --save
```

The preceding command will download and install Karma and the karma-coverage plugin into your `node_modules` folder. Then, it will add the entry to your `package.json devDependencies` property.

Karma configuration

Now, we need to adjust the Karma configuration file to include the correct files; since the project created in *Chapter 4*, *My Backbone Project*, uses CoffeeScript, we need to adjust the source location to use the compiled scripts.

Open `karma.conf.js` and add the following code:

```
module.exports = function (config) {
  config.set({
    basePath: '',
    frameworks: ['jasmine', 'requirejs'],
     files: [
    { pattern: 'app/bower_components/**/*.js', included: false },
      { pattern: '.tmp/scripts/**/*.js', included: false },
      { pattern: '.tmp/spec/**/*.js', included: false },
      'test/test-main.js'
    ],
    exclude: [],
    reporters: ['progress', 'coverage'],
    port: 9876,
    colors: true,
    logLevel: config.LOG_INFO,
```

```
      preprocessors: {
        '.tmp/scripts/**/*.js': ['coverage']
      },
      browsers: ['Chrome'],
      captureTimeout: 60000,
      autoWatch: false,
      client: {
        captureConsole: true,
        useIframe: false
      },
      singleRun: true
    });
};
```

The following actions are performed by the preceding code:

- At the top of the file, the module.exports property is set to a function that takes the config argument from Karma

- The config.set method is invoked by passing an object of settings to send to Karma

- The basePath property is set to an empty string

- The frameworks property is set to an array of libraries to include for testing

- The files property is set to an array of file objects that specify the files to index; here, we specify the bower_components directory, the compiled scripts and compiled test specs, and the test configuration main.js file

- The reporters property is set to an array of Karma reporters to use

- The port, colors, and logLevel properties are set to their default values

- The preprocessors property is set to an object of files and type of preprocessor; here, we specify the source of the compiled scripts to be run through the coverage preprocessor

- The browsers property is set to Google Chrome

- Then, we configure the client method to capture any console logs to the runner and set singleRun to true; so it will run and exit when finished

Configuring test-main.js

Now, we need to create a configuration file that will replicate the `app/scripts/main.coffee` file, and instead loop all files and then check if a test spec exists, pushing that file into an array that will be handed to Require.js when all is finished, which will in turn execute the specs. Create a new file by executing the following command:

```
$ touch test/test-main.js
```

Open the `test/test-main.js` file and add the following content:

```
var tests = Object.keys(window.__karma__.files).filter(function (file)
{
  var isTest = /.tmp\/spec.*.js/.test(file);
  if (isTest) {
    return file;
  }
});
requirejs.config({
  baseUrl: 'base/.tmp/scripts',
  shim: {
      "underscore": {
        "exports": "_"
      },
      "backbone": {
        "deps": [
          "underscore",
          "jquery"
        ],
        "exports": "Backbone"
      },
      "handlebars": {
        "exports": "Handlebars"
      }
  },
  paths: {
    "jquery": "../../app/bower_components/jquery/jquery",
    "backbone": "../../app/bower_components/backbone/backbone",
    "underscore": "../../app/bower_components/underscore/
      underscore",
    "handlebars": "../../app/bower_components/handlebars/
      handlebars",
```

```
    "app": "app"
},

// ask Require.js to load these files (all our tests)
deps: tests,

// start test run, once Require.js is done
callback: window.__karma__.start
});
```

The following actions are performed by the preceding code:

- At the top of the file, we declare a `tests` variable that will contain all the specs to run. It is set to the `Object.keys` method that will handle testing if the current file is indeed a test spec, and if it is, it will return that file, which pushes it into the files' array.

- Then, `requirejs` is configured with a new `baseUrl` property that will be the location of the source files. Since Karma places everything under the base, we need to adjust the URL accordingly.

- The `shim` and `paths` properties are set as normal to the same value as in the regular main script file.

- The `reps` property is set to the `files` array that will contain all the test specs to run.

- The `callback` property is set to the `start` method on the `karma` namespace object, which will invoke the runner and execute the tests.

Running tests

Now, we are ready to run the tests with Grunt, which will start the Karma runner and execute all the specs that are in the `test/spec` directory. Open the terminal and execute the following command:

```
$ grunt test
```

The preceding command will do the following tasks:

- It will run the test task that will clean the `.tmp` directory
- It will compile the CoffeeScript's source and spec files
- Then, it will launch Karma, which in turn will execute the specs

Code coverage report

Now, we are ready to view the code coverage that Karma generated after running the tests; Karma uses Istanbul for instrumenting and displaying the coverage reports. The reports are created in the root of the project in a folder named `coverage`, inside the folder will be another folder with the same name as the browser on which we ran our tests.

Open the `index.html` file in a browser of your choice to view the code coverage. You should see something similar to the following screenshot if all went well:

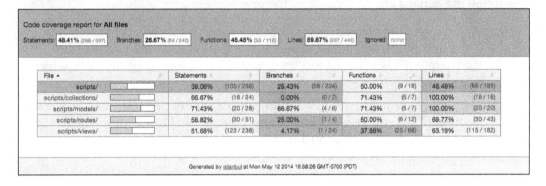

Self-test questions

1. How do you start and update the Selenium WebDriver when using Protractor in your project?

2. What npm module enables your project to generate code coverage from unit tests?

Summary

In this chapter, we covered a lot of things. We began with setting up a Node RESTful server that talks to a MongoDB database and returns JSON to the browser. We set up Protractor with an Angular application to cover the e2e tests that are needed as an application gets larger. We also set up Karma to handle testing our specs and generating code coverage on a Backbone application that uses Require.js and CoffeeScript. Finding the correct solution to a problem can sometimes be a difficult task, but with patience and persistence, anything can be done; take this chapter as a welcome to writing better unit tests and creating projects with outstanding code coverage.

Yeoman Resources

This chapter will include often-used commands when using Grunt, Bower, and Yo, as well as the other tools and technologies used in this book; it will serve as a reference for developers when using tools in the Yeoman workflow and also includes installation details to set up the development environment.

Reference guides

As using the Yeoman workflow tools includes several different commands, let's have a look at the reference commands and documentation.

Yo – the scaffolding tool

Yo is a lightening-fast scaffolding tool that runs in the Node.js environment.

Usage

The Yo tool is invoked from the command line as follows:

```
$ yo [generator] [args] [options]


General options:
  -h, --help      # Print generator's options and usage
  -f, --force     # Overwrite files that already exist
```

 For more information on Yo, visit http://goo.gl/ft8YFz.

Bower – the package tool

Bower is a package manager for the web.

Usage

The Bower tool is invoked from the command line as follows:

```
$ bower [command] [args] [options]
```

Commands

The Bower commands available are as follows:

Command	Description
cache	This manages the Bower cache
help	This displays help information about Bower
home	This opens a package homepage into your favorite browser
info	This provides information on a particular package
init	This interactively creates a bower.json file
install	This installs a package locally
link	This symlinks a package folder
list	This lists local packages
lookup	This looks up a package URL by name
prune	This removes local extraneous packages
register	This registers a package
search	This searches for a package by name
update	This updates a local package
uninstall	This removes a local package

Options

The Bower options available are as follows:

Option	Description
-f, --force	This makes various commands more forceful
-j, --json	This outputs consumable JSON
-l, --log-level	This lists what level of logs to report
-o, --offline	This does not hit the network
-q, --quiet	This provides only important output information

Option	Description
-s, --silent	This does not output anything, besides errors
-V, --verbose	This makes output more verbose
--allow-root	This allows running commands as root

 For more information on Bower, visit `http://goo.gl/x0RuZ6.`

Grunt – the build tool

Grunt is a JavaScript task runner that runs in the Node.js environment.

Usage

The Grunt tool is invoked from the command line as follows:

```
$ grunt [task] [options]
```

Options

The Grunt options available are as follows:

Option	Description
-h, --help	This displays the help text
-d, --debug	This enables debugging mode for tasks that support it
-f, --force	This provides a way to force your way past warnings
-v, --verbose	This enables detailed logging to be displayed during execution
-V, --version	This prints the Grunt version and combines it with --verbose for more information
--base	This specifies an alternate base path
--no-color	This disables colored output
--gruntfile	This specifies an alternate Gruntfile
--stack	This prints a stack trace when exiting with a warning or fatal error
--tasks	This lists additional directory paths to scan for task and extra files
--npm	This lists npm-installed Grunt plugins to scan for task and extra files
--no-write	This disables writing files (dry run)
--completion	This outputs shell autocompletion rules

[For more information on Grunt, visit `http://goo.gl/XA9qnz`.]

Git

Git is a version control system to manage a project's code base.

Usage

To use the Git tool, the usage is as follows:

```
$ git [command] [args] [options]
```

Commands

The Git commands available are as follows:

Command	Description
add	This adds file contents to the index
bisect	This finds by binary search the change that introduced a bug
branch	This lists, creates, or deletes branches
checkout	This checks out a branch or paths to the working tree
clone	This clones a repository into a new directory
commit	This records changes to the repository
diff	This shows changes between commits, commit and working tree, and so on
fetch	This downloads objects and refs from another repository
grep	This prints lines that match a pattern
init	This creates an empty Git repository or reinitializes an existing one
log	This shows commit logs
merge	This joins two or more development histories together
mv	This moves or renames a file, directory, or symlink
pull	This fetches from and merges with another repository or a local branch
push	This updates remote refs along with associated objects
rebase	This integrates changes from two different branches
reset	This resets the current HEAD to the specified state
rm	This removes files from the working tree and from the index

Command	Description
show	This shows various types of objects
status	This shows the working tree status
tag	This creates, lists, deletes, or verifies a tag object signed with GPG

Jasmine – behavior-driven JavaScript

Jasmine is a behavior-driven testing framework for JavaScript programming language.

Structure of a suite

Jasmine uses the `describe` and `it` methods to structure test suites, as follows:

```
describe("colors", function() {
    describe("red", function() {
        var red;
        beforeEach(function() {
            red = new Color("red");
        });
        afterEach(function() {
            red = null;
        });
        it("has the correct value", function() {
            expect(red.hex).toEqual("FF0000");
        });
        it("makes orange when mixed with yellow", function() {
            var yellow = new Color("yellow");
            var orange = new Color("orange");
            expect(red.mix(yellow)).toEqual(orange);
        });
    });
});
```

Matchers

The available Jasmine matchers are as follows:

Method	Description
expect(x).toEqual(n)	This checks whether x is equal to n
expect(x).toBe(n)	This checks whether two objects are the same
expect(x).toBeTruthy()	This checks whether the value of x is truthy (not just true)
expect(x).toBeFalsy()	This checks whether the value of x is falsy (not just false)
expect(x).toContain(n)	This checks whether the value of x contains value n

Method	Description
expect(x).toBeDefined()	This checks whether the value of x is defined
expect(x).toBeUndefined()	This checks whether the value of x is undefined
expect(x).toBeNull()	This checks whether the value of x is null
expect(x).toBeNaN()	This checks whether the value of x is NaN
expect(x).toBeCloseTo(n)	This checks the decimal proximity of x
expect(x).toMatch(n)	This checks whether the value of x matches a given regular expression
expect(x).toThrow(e)	This checks whether the x function throws an error
expect(x).not.toEqual(n)	This checks the x inverse of the following matcher

Spy matchers

The available Jasmine spy matchers are as follows:

Method	Description
expect(x).toHaveBeenCalled()	This passes if x is a spy and has been called
expect(x).toHaveBeenCalledWith(args)	This passes if x is a spy and has been called with args
expect(x).not.toHaveBeenCalled()	This passes if x is a spy and was not called
expect(x).not. toHaveBeenCalledWith(args)	This passes if x is a spy and has not been called with args
spyOn(x, 'method').andCallThrough()	This spies on AND invokes the original spied-on function
spyOn(x, 'method').andReturn(args)	This returns args when the spy method is invoked
spyOn(x, 'method').andThrow(exception)	This throws the passed exception when the method is invoked
spyOn(x, 'method').andCallFake(fn)	This invokes the passed fn function when spy is invoked

Reserved words

The reserved words in Jasmine are as follows:

Word	Description
jasmine	This is the global variable for the Jasmine instance
describe(description, function)	This groups a related set of specs
it(description, function)	This invokes the function for test spec

Word	Description
expect(x)	This is an expectation that takes the expected value
beforeEach(function)	This makes the function invoke before each spec in suite
afterEach(function)	This makes the function invoke after each spec in suite
runs(function)	This starts an asynchronous operation
waits(condition)	This waits for condition
waitsFor(function, message, timeout)	This waits until the function returns `true` within a specified timeout
spyOn	This stubs the function and tracks calls and arguments
xdescribe	This marks a suite as pending and skips
xit	This marks a spec as pending and skips

 For more information on Jasmine, visit `http://goo.gl/2tpIUV`.

Installation guides

In order to take full advantage of the Yeoman Workflow, you need to set up your development environment. The following tools are required for this book's projects and code examples.

Installing Git

There are many ways to install and run Git. Let's take a look at the installation steps for both Mac and Windows operating systems.

Installing Git on Windows

To install Git on Windows, follow these steps:

1. Visit `http://git-scm.com/downloads`, and click on the **Windows** link.
2. Run the `.exe` file that was downloaded.
3. Follow the installation steps, and Git will be installed as a command-line utility.

Installing Git on Mac

To install Git on Mac, follow these steps:

1. Visit `http://git-scm.com/downloads`, and click on the **Mac OS X** link.
2. Run the `.dmg` file that was downloaded.
3. Follow the installation steps, and Git will be installed as a command-line utility.

Once Git is installed, you can test `git` by executing the following command:

```
$ git --version
```

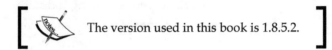 The version used in this book is 1.8.5.2.

Installing Node.js and npm

As npm comes bundled with Node.js, installing Node.js will install npm.

Installing Node on Windows

The following steps will cover the installation of `npm` on Windows through the Node installer:

1. Download the `.msi` installer located at `http://nodejs.org/download/`.
2. Run the `.msi` installer to install Node and npm.
3. Follow the installation steps, and npm will be installed as a command-line utility.

Installing Node on Mac

The following steps will cover the installation of npm on Mac through the Node installer:

1. Download the `.pkg` installer located at `http://nodejs.org/download`.
2. Run the `.pkg` installer to install Node and npm.
3. Follow the installation steps, and npm will be installed as a command-line utility.

Once Node is installed, you can test Node and npm by executing the following command:

```
$ node -v && npm -v
```

 The version used in this book is Node 0.10.28 and npm 1.4.9.

Installing Yo

As Yo runs in the Node.js environment, you should already have Node and npm installed.

Installing Yo on Mac/Windows

Once npm is installed, you can install Yo globally using the following command:

```
$ npm install -g yo
```

Once Yo is installed, you can test Yo by executing the following command:

```
$ yo -v
```

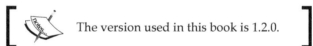 The version used in this book is 1.2.0.

Installing Grunt

As Grunt runs in the Node.js environment, you should already have Node and npm installed.

Installing Grunt on Mac/Windows

Once npm is installed, you can install Grunt globally using the following command:

```
$ npm install -g grunt-cli
```

Once Grunt is installed, you can test Grunt by executing the following command:

```
$ grunt --v
```

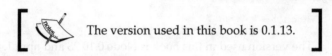 The version used in this book is 0.1.13.

Installing Bower

As Bower runs in the Node.js environment, you should already have Node and npm installed.

Installing Bower on Mac/Windows

Once npm is installed, you can install Bower globally using the following command:

```
$ npm install -g bower
```

Once Bower is installed, you can test Bower by executing the following command:

```
$ bower -v
```

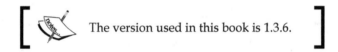 The version used in this book is 1.3.6.

Self-test answers

The following sections are the answers to the questions that the user should be able to answer after reading each chapter.

Chapter 1, Modern Workflows for Modern Webapps

1. The four most popular Yeoman generators are as follows:

    ° **generator-angular**: This is for AngularJS applications

    ° **generator-backbone**: This is for Backbone.js applications

    ° **generator-ember**: This is for Ember.js applications

    ° **generator-webapp**: This is for generic web applications

2. The three core tools used in Yeoman are as follows:

    ° **Yo**: This is the build tool

    ° **Bower**: This is the package tool

    ° **Grunt**: This is the build tool

3. The general developer workflow when using Yeoman is as follows:

```
$ yo        # scaffold project
$ bower     # manage dependencies
$ grunt     # preview, test, build
```

4. Yeoman requires and runs in the Node.js environment on either the Windows, Mac, or Linux platform.

5. Addy Osmani and Paul Irish are the major contributors behind the creation of Yeoman.

Chapter 2, Getting Started

1. The names of at least three Yeoman generators are generator-node, generator-angular, and generator-ember.

2. The angular:route subgenerator in the generator-angular package will create a template and controller, and wire the named route to the applications router (`app/scripts/app.js`).

3. The default test framework for the Backbone generator is Mocha, which is a feature-rich JavaScript test framework that runs on Node and the browser.

4. The `--coffee` option is available in all four generators:

    ° generator-webapp

    ° generator-angular

    ° generator-backbone

    ° generator-ember

5. The `search generator-` will search npm for all packages with `generator-` in the name.

6. The ember:model subgenerator will create a model, controller, route, view, and template for the passed name argument.

7. The default test framework for a scaffolded Ember project is Mocha.

Chapter 3, My Angular Project

1. Angular supports two-way data binding using the {{ }} double mustache syntax.

2. The `angular.module` method is used to define Angular modules.

3. The `directive` module should be used when creating a reusable UI component.

4. The Jasmine framework is the default testing framework.

5. The `service` module should be used when creating reusable business logic.

Chapter 4, My Backbone Project

1. The library that Backbone.js heavily depends on is Underscore.js.

2. All Backbone classes extend the `Backbone.Event` class.

3. The Require.js option is only available in the generator-backbone project.

4. The `Backbone.Model` class provides basic functionality to manage changes to the model data.

5. The `Backbone.Collection` class provides functionality to manage an ordered set of models.

Chapter 5, My Ember Project

1. The Handlebars library is built into Ember.

2. The `EmberData` class (`DS`) object provides access to various types of prescient storage options.

3. Two things that uniquely identify records are as follows:
   ° A model type
   ° A globally unique ID

4. Models can use the `hasMany` or `belongsTo` property to specify what the value is when creating the model's definition.

5. To find a single record, you pass a second argument to the `find` method, which is the unique identifier of the model, as follows:

```
this.model.find('post', 1);
```

6. To delete a model, you invoke the `deleteRecord()` method on a model instance as follows:

```
this.get('model').deleteRecord();
```

7. To link a view action to a controller or route, you use the `{{action 'name'}}` helper in your view template. The `name` parameter is the name of the action you wish to invoke. To pass arguments to the action handler, just pass in the arguments after the name of the action as follows:

```
<p>
    <button {{action "select" post}}>View</button
        {{ post.title }}
</p>
```

Chapter 6, Custom Generators

1. To invoke a subgenerator, use the `generator:sub-generator` command, where the generator is the name of the Yeoman generator and subgenerator is the name of the subgenerator.

2. The default templating library that Yeoman uses is the Underscore.js template method.

3. The two types of generators are basic and advanced. A basic generator simply copies files from one location to another, and an advanced generator uses prompts and dynamic templates when writing files to their destination.

4. The two types of tests that are created by default when invoking the Yeoman generator-generator are as follows:

    ° The `test-creation.js` test, which tests whether the generator can create the expected files

    ° The `test-load.js` test, which tests whether the generator can be loaded into the system without blowing up

5. The Mocha library is used to test Yeoman generators.

6. Yeoman uses the Inquery.js library for its command prompts.

7. The four methods that are created on the custom generator object are `init`, `askFor`, `files`, and `app`; they are explained as follows:

    ° The `app` function is responsible for creating all the applications' project files

    ° The `files` function is responsible for creating all the application-specific files

    ° The `askFor` function is responsible for prompting the user with questions and storing values

    ° The `init` function is responsible for setting up initial variables and other initializing methods

8. To create a subgenerator, you extend the `yeoman.generators.NamedBase` class with your own subgenerator-specific methods as follows:

```
var MySubGenerator = yeoman.generators.NamedBase.extend(
        init: function(){},
        files: function(){}
    );
```

Chapter 7, Custom Libraries

1. A package manager is a tool to automate the process of installing, upgrading, configuring, and managing dependencies for projects.

2. A command-line interface is a way for developers to interact with a system using text commands.

3. To register a package on Bower, use the `register` command by passing the name and URL of the package as follows:

```
$ bower register [name] [url]
```

Chapter 8, Tasks with Grunt

1. The `grunt -h` command is used to list all of the available tasks defined in the relative `Gruntfile.js` file.

2. The three most common Grunt tasks are `grunt`, `test`, and `serve`.

3. Grunt runs in the Node.js environment and is invoked from the command line.

4. To execute a target task in Grunt, you use the `task:target` syntax that will execute the named task in the named target.

5. To register a new Grunt task, you use the `grunt.registerTask` method by passing in the name of the task and the array of subtasks to execute. Additionally, you can pass in a callback function instead of the array, and this function will be invoked by passing the target as the argument. This allows you to conditionally execute tasks based on what the target is.

6. To install a new Grunt task, you must first install it using npm; use the `npm install grunt-contrib-jshint --save-dev` command to install the plugin and save it to your `package.json` file.

7. The alternatives to Grunt would be Ant, Make, Jake, Rake, SBT, and other build-type tools.

Chapter 9, Yeoman Tips and Tricks

1. To start and update the Selenium WebDriver, you would use the `webdriver-manager` command and either start or update the Selenium WebDriver.

2. The `karma-coverage` module allows your project to generate detailed code coverage reports using Istanbul. To add coverage, you need to modify your `karma.conf.js` file and add the settings that configure the module as follows:

```
reporters: ['progress', 'coverage'],
preprocessors: {
    '.tmp/scripts//*.js': ['coverage']
},
```

Summary

This appendix covered all of the available options and commands for the tools used in the Yeoman workflow. It also covered installation details for each of the tools.

Index

findOne method 174
find(selector, context) method 117
footer element 54

G

generator-angular
  about 31
  conclusion 36
  example usage 32
  features 32
  installing 32
  options 32
  previewing 35
  subgenerators 33
  using 32
generator-backbone
  about 36
  conclusion 39
  example usage 37
  features 36
  installing 36
  options 37
  previewing 38
  subgenerators 37, 41
  using 36
generator-ember
  conclusion 42
  example usage 40
  features 40
  installing 40
  options 40
  previewing 42
  using 40
generators
  about 27
  URL 29
generator-webapp
  about 29
  conclusion 31
  example usage 30
  features 29
  installing 29
  options 30
  previewing 30
  using 29
GET route, RESTful Node.js server 220, 221

Git
  about 242
  commands 242
  installing 245
  installing, on Mac 246
  installing, on Windows 245
  URL 245
  usage 242
Git attributes
  URL 151
Git commands
  add 242
  bisect 242
  branch 242
  checkout 242
  clone 242
  commit 242
  diff 242
  fetch 242
  grep 242
  init 242
  log 242
  merge 242
  mv 242
  pull 242
  push 242
  rebase 242
  reset 242
  rm 242
  show 243
  status 243
  tag 243
Git ignore file
  URL 152
Grunt
  about 7, 241
  adding, to project 208
  alias tasks, creating 204
  basic tasks, registering 205
  Gruntfile.js file 203
  installing 200, 247
  installing, on Mac 247
  installing, on Windows 247
  multiple target tasks 204
  options 201, 241
  package.json file 202, 203
  setting up 202

Thank you for buying
Learning Yeoman

About Packt Publishing

Packt, pronounced 'packed', published its first book "*Mastering phpMyAdmin for Effective MySQL Management*" in April 2004 and subsequently continued to specialize in publishing highly focused books on specific technologies and solutions.

Our books and publications share the experiences of your fellow IT professionals in adapting and customizing today's systems, applications, and frameworks. Our solution based books give you the knowledge and power to customize the software and technologies you're using to get the job done. Packt books are more specific and less general than the IT books you have seen in the past. Our unique business model allows us to bring you more focused information, giving you more of what you need to know, and less of what you don't.

Packt is a modern, yet unique publishing company, which focuses on producing quality, cutting-edge books for communities of developers, administrators, and newbies alike. For more information, please visit our website: www.packtpub.com.

About Packt Open Source

In 2010, Packt launched two new brands, Packt Open Source and Packt Enterprise, in order to continue its focus on specialization. This book is part of the Packt Open Source brand, home to books published on software built around Open Source licenses, and offering information to anybody from advanced developers to budding web designers. The Open Source brand also runs Packt's Open Source Royalty Scheme, by which Packt gives a royalty to each Open Source project about whose software a book is sold.

Writing for Packt

We welcome all inquiries from people who are interested in authoring. Book proposals should be sent to author@packtpub.com. If your book idea is still at an early stage and you would like to discuss it first before writing a formal book proposal, contact us; one of our commissioning editors will get in touch with you.

We're not just looking for published authors; if you have strong technical skills but no writing experience, our experienced editors can help you develop a writing career, or simply get some additional reward for your expertise.

Getting Started with Grunt: The JavaScript Task Runner

ISBN: 978-1-78398-062-8   Paperback: 132 pages

A hands-on approach to mastering the fundamentals of Grunt

1. Gain insight on the core concepts of Grunt, Node.js, and npm to get started with Grunt.

2. Learn how to install, configure, run, and customize Grunt.

3. Example-driven and filled with tips to help you create custom Grunt tasks.

Mastering Grunt

ISBN: 978-1-78398-092-5   Paperback: 110 pages

Master this powerful build automation tool to streamline your application development

1. Master the development of your web applications by combining Grunt with an army of other useful tools.

2. Learn about the key tasks behind DevOps integration and automation so you can utilize Grunt in a team-working environment.

3. Accelerate your web development abilities by employing best practices, including SEO, page speed optimization, and responsive design.

Please check **www.PacktPub.com** for information on our titles

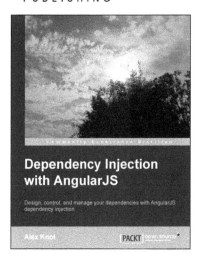

Dependency Injection with AngularJS

ISBN: 978-1-78216-656-6   Paperback: 78 pages

Design, control, and manage your dependencies with AngularJS dependency injection

1. Understand the concept of dependency injection.

2. Isolate units of code during testing JavaScript using Jasmine.

3. Create reusable components in AngularJS.

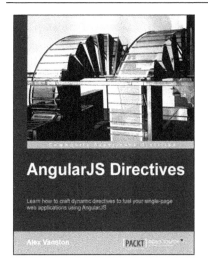

AngularJS Directives

ISBN: 978-1-78328-033-9   Paperback: 110 pages

Learn how to craft dynamic directives to fuel your single-page web applications using AngularJS

1. Learn how to build an AngularJS directive.

2. Create extendable modules for plug-and-play usability.

3. Build apps that react in real time to changes in your data model.

Please check **www.PacktPub.com** for information on our titles